Professional Collaboration with Parents of Children with Disabilities

Professional Collaboration with Parents of Children with Disabilities

LOUISE PORTER PhD, MGiftedEd, DipEd
Flinders University of South Australia

AND

SUSAN MCKENZIE PhD, MSpec.Ed, BECE, DipT
Murdoch University, Perth, Western Australia

W

WHURR PUBLISHERS
LONDON AND PHILADELPHIA

© 2000 Whurr Publishers
First published 2000 by
Whurr Publishers Ltd
19b Compton Terrace, London N1 2UN, England and
325 Chestnut Street, Philadelphia PA 1906, USA

British Library Cataloguing in Publication Data
A catalogue record for this book is available from the
British Library.

ISBN: 1 86156 174 1

Printed and bound in the UK by Athenaeum Press Ltd,
Gateshead, Tyne & Wear

Contents

Dedications

We dedicate this book to our own families, without whose steadfast
support we could not have produced this work.
We also thank the many parents who have been willing
to share with us their hopes and dreams,
their ups and downs and their personal triumphs.
Without *them*, this book would not have been written.

Chapter 1
The collaborative relationship

> Parents take their child home after professionals complete their services and parents continue providing the care for the larger portion of the child's waking hours . . . No matter how skilled professionals are, or how loving parents are, each cannot achieve alone what the two parties, working hand-in-hand, can accomplish together.
>
> Peterson and Cooper (1989: 208, 229)

Key points

- As a professional, you are accountable not only to the children with whom you work, but also to their parents as consumers of your service.
- When you collaborate with parents, their child's development is optimized, the parents feel confident of their skills, and they are more likely in future to choose to be involved with professionals.
- The parent-professional relationship has evolved over the past few decades and parents' roles within that have altered. Recently, the emphasis has been on empowering parents to care for their child. The next phase of this evolution will be for professionals not to assume that parents *need* us to empower them, but that we must simply avoid disempowering them.
- It is neither necessary nor productive for professionals to dominate the parent-professional relationship. If we regard parents as employing us to deliver the services they seek for their child, we will avoid their becoming dependent on professional service providers, and will attract all the benefits of a collaborative relationship.

Introduction

In your role as a teacher or some other paediatric professional, your primary role is to teach or work with children. This is quite clear: your responsibilities are towards the children in your care. But what affects the

1

children in your class (or in your care) goes home with them and reverberates in their families. And some of what happens at home comes in with the children when they start their day with you.

This means that your role is more complicated than simply relating with children. But this is not a negative thing, because most parents support and love their children, encouraging the children's learning and development. Without the parents, your job would be harder. Sometimes, however, families are not managing to support their children. In these cases, it is easy to see them as a hindrance to your work with their child.

In this book, we aim to help turn this view around. Parents are on your team. They want the best for their child, just as you do. But, historically, professional practice implied that the way to get the best for children was for parents to clear the scene and let professionals get on with doing their job.

These days, this is not going to happen. Not just because there are parents who do not *want* to leave you to get on with it, but because it simply *is not possible* for you to work solely with a child, without what you do affecting that child's parents and what the parents do affecting what you can achieve with their child. You, the child, and the family are intermeshed. We would be deluding ourselves to pretend otherwise. It is not just a matter of providing an excellent service to children. We are accountable to their families too.

Our stance in this book is that we work with parents because they are their children's main source of support. When families are functioning successfully, children can function successfully. When you can support the family, you increase the chances of having a positive effect on the child (Dunst et al. 1994).

This is not to say that you have to assume that when a child in your care has special educational needs, the parents too will have special needs. As this chapter will describe, it might simply mean making sure that the service that you offer their child – and therefore that you offer parents indirectly – does not undermine or have negative outcomes for them.

The concept of collaboration is built on systems theory which says that families – and any other ongoing groups – have members who are connected to each other. All family members are part of a whole rather than separate individuals. This means that what affects one person in the family will affect them all. Like the ripples that spread outwards when you drop a pebble into a pond, the person nearest the disturbance is most affected, but the ripples spread out to all parts of the system, affecting peripheral members less significantly but nevertheless still noticeably.

Because all family members are interconnected, even when your prime task is to work directly with children, it will be important that you maintain parents' confidence in their ability to make decisions for their child. When you can support them in this role, they are ultimately better able to attend to the needs of all their family, including the child who is your professional focus.

Rationale for collaboration with parents

We believe that the interests of a child who has a disability and his or her entire family are best met by taking every family member's needs into account, by promoting the whole family's healthy functioning and maintaining the parents' confidence in their ability to care for all their children.

Parents and professionals each bring some useful and complementary strengths to their relationships (Hamre-Nietupski et al. 1988). (These are summarized in Table 1.1.) There is a place for both parents' and professionals' views of children and their needs (Blodgett 1971). There is no need for parents and professionals to compete with each other: they can complement each other and, in so doing, enrich the picture of the child's and family's needs and skills.

Table 1.1: Contributions and responsibilities of parents and professionals in their care of a child with a disability

Contribution	Responsibility
Parents	
Commitment to whole child.	To make decisions in the child's interests.
Knowledge of child.	To inform professionals of the child's needs and preferences.
High emotional involvement in the child.	To balance the child's needs with those of all family members.
Direct experience of having a child with special needs.	
Professionals	
Knowledge of disability.	To listen to parents' knowledge and to recognise limitations in professional expertise.
Knowledge of service system.	To refer children and families to other services if their needs extend beyond one's own role.
Short-term commitment to the child and family.	To offer a service that advances the interests of the child and family, balanced with one's responsibilities to one's employer and the wider community.

As a professional, you bring to your relationship with parents your experience of the service system; your expertise with professional literature and research; and your knowledge of how your particular discipline can contribute to a child's or family's well-being.

For their part, parents will have a strong commitment to their children and families and knowledge about how best to meet family and individual needs. They can contribute their expertise about their own children; their informed observations of their children over a long period of time and in many circumstances; their knowledge of their children's needs; commitment to voicing these needs on their children's behalf; and their knowledge of what is best for their family. In recognition of these contributions, the drive towards collaboration with parents is based on a number of assumptions (Dale 1996; Sebastian 1989):

- Parents have the most important and enduring relationship with their children.
- Children learn more from their home environment than from any other setting.
- Parents have more detailed knowledge than professionals about their child across time and in a variety of settings; moreover, this knowledge is more personal and in-depth than professionals can usually access.
- Thus, professionals need parents' input if they are to do their job effectively.
- Parents' involvement in their child's education contributes to children's positive attitudes to learning and to themselves as learners (Raban 1997).
- Parental involvement in their child's education promotes mutual respect and understanding between the home and other settings such as the school or clinic.
- Parents can make valuable contributions to their child's schooling.
- Accountability is more open when parents are involved in their child's programme.
- Some parents need extra support and guidance to understand and cater for the needs of their child with a disability.
- Unless professionals work alongside parents, not only are both parties unable to partake of the benefits of their partnership, but professionals' work can actually undermine parents' abilities (Trivette et al. 1996).

Not all parents will be able to articulate adequately the special needs of their children, while others will have considerable skills for doing so because they have had a good deal of prior experience advocating for their children's needs. From their experience with negotiating the service system, many parents will come to know the system better than some professionals do and will have built up particular skills in dealing with service organizations. It is also likely that they will know more about their child's particular disability than many professionals and certainly they will be experts on the goals and aspirations of their own child and family. Therefore it is important that their knowledge, skills and experience are valued.

There can be many benefits of collaborating with parents (Cunningham 1985). The first is that programmes that involve parents are more successful than those which exclude them. Whether in early intervention (Cook et al. 2000) or when students are making the transition from high school to adult life, parental involvement is the main determinant of success (Morningstar et al. 1995). Parents' involvement leads to improved developmental outcomes for the child and reduced family stress.

Through their participation in their child's programme, parents may receive information that will help them know what to expect of their child, the programme and the future. They may gain some specialist skills for assisting their child's development. Both this information and an expanded repertoire of skills will give them confidence in their parenting role and empower them to make decisions. This can be especially valuable at the time immediately following the child's diagnosis (Hanson 1987). Success in working with professionals will also encourage parents to ask for support again in the future if problems arise. Finally, their involvement can help to overcome any feelings of isolation that parents may have been experiencing, and sensitive professional involvement will remind them to attend to their own needs and those of other family members.

Meanwhile, you can learn from parents about what works for them at home with their child. This information can save a good deal of frustration and wasted time as parents can recount their child's history prior to your involvement, on the basis of which you may be able to assess what interventions are likely to be most successful in future.

The evolving parent-professional relationship

Although working with parents has been an aim of professional services for much of their history, over time changing views of disability, of parents, of professionals, and of their relationship have resulted in a move away from relationships characterised by professional dominance towards collaboration with parents.

Professional dominance

In the past, the community saw professionals as having high status by virtue of their specialized knowledge, to which only they had access (Thompson et al. 1997). Lay people deferred to professionals' opinions – both within and outside of their specialty areas – and did not question their judgement. Meanwhile, the 'experts' themselves expected nothing less, assuming that parents knew little – and, sometimes, needed to know little – about their child.

This was also the age of superstition about disabilities, which gave rise to what Dunst and colleagues (1988) call a moralist perspective on intervention. This is guided by the dual maxims that, in life 'You get what you deserve' and 'You deserve what you get'. These beliefs allowed outsiders to blame parents for their child's disability. A few parents continue to work under this assumption – that their child's disability is a punishment for their former 'sins' and that, therefore, they should make no attempt to improve their child's condition as that would be a denial of their 'just punishment' for some act or omission that they regret. Although this attitude has never been a formal part of professional intervention with children who have disabilities, in these early days, some parents were accused of causing particular disabilities. For instance, autism was once thought to be caused by 'refrigerator mothers' whose coldness to their child was said to cause the child's social development to stall, when, in fact, the mother's observed unresponsiveness was a *result* of her autistic child's not returning her affection. (A modern example of this is the misconception that ADHD is caused by 'poor' parenting.)

With this moralist perspective as a background, professional services were put in place to correct deficiencies in children's home experiences. The medical model dominated such remedial services (even when there was nothing medically wrong with a child who had a disability). Some professionals felt that they had to rescue or 'save' children from 'deficient' parents, with a high proportion of these parents coming from non-majority cultural backgrounds.

Parents themselves were dismissed as irrelevant to their children's learning. At that time, children with disabilities were routinely placed in institutions and parents were advised to 'go home and forget' their child. Those who wished to visit were sometimes denied access to their institutionalized sons or daughters, in the belief that parents exerted a negative influence or 'unsettled' their offspring.

Both the moralist and medical models can give rise to oppositional encounters between parents and the professionals who are supposed to be helping them (Dunst et al. 1988). This arises because of the either-or thinking of these perspectives in which one party (the parents) is defined as wrong and professionals are seen to be right.

To illustrate how easy it is for parents to defer to professional judgement, a personal story might help. I (Louise) was the parent of a six-month-old child. When she began centre-based care, the caregiver told me that her prolonged distress and crying was a tantrum and that she was doing it to get attention (as if that were not a legitimate goal for a baby). I almost deferred to this caregiver's opinion – until I remembered that *I* was the child psychologist, that *I* had 15 years' experience specializing in young children's behavioural difficulties and, moreover, *I* was her parent, with 100 times more contact with her – and immeasurably more intimate knowledge of her – than this caregiver had.

It struck me how my role as a parent had almost made me willing to surrender the first two bodies of knowledge to someone who was less qualified than I. Imagine how tempting it must be for parents who are 'unqualified' to deny what they know about their children in the face of a contrary professional opinion.

Communicating with parents

As notions of dominance receded, the next phase in relationships between parents and professionals limited the responsibility of professionals to *communicating* with parents about the programme, making them the recipients of professional opinion. Parents remained passive and compliant, while professionals still held the dominant role as experts who 'knew what was best' for children. They were expected to make the educational decisions and interpret them to parents, who in turn were expected not to question these.

Cooperation with parents

After the focus on communicating, the next advance in the relationship between professionals and parents was to involve parents in their child's schooling or other programme, but only when they were available to take part and only on the school or agency's terms. This cooperative relationship is more reciprocal than the one-way flow of information from the school to home, but it does not necessarily imply a high level of participation (Waters 1996), and might comprise only token involvement such as organizing an excursion or helping to raise funds. In a cooperative relationship, parents and professionals might simply work together but mainly in parallel with each other.

Coordination

Coordination requires some joint planning and sharing of information. As such, it represents a move away from the view of professionals as experts and aims to provide supportive relationships, rather than taking the oppositional stance of the moralist and medical models (Dunst et al. 1988). In the early days of coordination, professionals still oversaw or coordinated the child's programme and so could dictate parents' roles, sometimes imposing formal teaching roles on them, for instance, or offering parents training so that they could learn the skills that the professionals determined the parents needed to acquire.

Collaboration

The most recent emphasis is on collaboration between parents and professionals. Collaboration means that power is shared (Daka-Mulwanda et al. 1995), with parents and professionals jointly determining goals and planning strategies with each other (Friend and Cook 1996; Hostetler 1991).

However, while emphasizing the equal status of parents and professionals, this more inclusive relationship style does not imply sameness of roles. Professionals may deliver most of the child's services, while parents might not participate on a day-to-day basis in their child's programme (Arthur et al. 1996). Just as parents of children without disabilities are free to choose a low level of involvement in their child's education, the same choice might be made by parents whose children have special needs.

Under this model, although the community continues to respect professionals' specialist knowledge, there is also a recognition that professionals do not know everything. At the same time, lay people are becoming astute consumers in all arenas, and are more willing to ask questions of their advisers. This does not diminish their respect for what specialists do know, but is built on the awareness that a lot of professional practice does not come from proven theory but from experience. And even the most experienced professionals can see things in routine ways, do things 'because that's the way we've always done it' or forget to question standard practices. Professional opinion might be only that: opinion.

Collaboration, then, is a philosophical stance which implies a shared responsibility for decisions about the care and education of children (Arthur et al. 1996; Fleet and Clyde 1993). The parents may or may not take an active part in delivering services to children, according to their desires and other commitments, while the professional's role is to support parents in their chosen role, without defining for them what form that should take. Thus, collaboration is a style or a state of mind, a way of communicating and working with parents: it does not imply the extent of parents' involvement in the day-to-day care or education of their child.

Tinworth (1994: 28–9) describes a family-centred approach to working with parents:

> In such a model, services build from family needs and . . . empower the family to make informed choices and control the direction of the service. The approach is sensitive to the family's values, beliefs and aspirations and seeks to construct a service that [they] can identify with and be energized by.

In a collaborative working relationship, the interactions between professionals and parents are likely to be aimed at helping families in a practical sense to achieve their own goals and meet family needs. Collaborative relationships emphasize the inherent strengths within families and value the positive contributions that individuals with disabilities make to their families.

The goal of this form of parent-professional relationship as just defined is to support the whole family system in its overall functioning so that it can negotiate the ongoing and changing developmental challenges of the child and family. The stated aim has been to *empower* parents to obtain the services that their child and family need (Turnbull and Turnbull 1997), without developing in parents the reliance and dependency on formal support that comes about when their confidence has been undermined by outside experts.

A second goal is to empower professionals to provide these services. Professionals will be empowered when they know how to secure relevant services to meet a child's needs, can collaborate with other service providers and, when appropriate to their role, can deliver an effective service themselves.

A third goal is to empower young people with disabilities by listening to their aspirations and suggestions about how they would like services to help them achieve those (Turnbull and Turnbull 1997).

In this way, *mutual* empowerment results from collaboration between families and professionals. It is both an outcome and a process by which individuals gain mastery over their lives (Dempsey 1994). It promotes parents' and professionals' decision-making and problem-solving skills and helps them to locate and procure the resources that they require (Dunst et al. 1988).

The next phase: beyond empowerment

This trend towards shared power is dynamic or ongoing. We believe that it has to go one step further: we want to go beyond the notion of empowerment, as it could be seen to imply that parents presently lack the power and skills for meeting the needs of their son or daughter. We believe that it is not up to us to assume that parents *need* us to empower them: it is simply up to us to make sure that we do not *dis*empower them by our efforts at 'helping'. Our approach assumes that parents already have many skills and will use them when their circumstances permit.

Roles of parents

In parallel with the changing relationship between parents and professionals, the role of parents has also undergone several shifts. Turnbull and Turnbull (1997: 12) summarize these changes in parental roles over the past century as occurring in four dimensions:

- from viewing parents as the source of the child's problem, to being its major solution;
- from insisting on passive roles to expecting active ones;
- from viewing families as a mother-child dyad to recognizing the presence and needs of all members;
- from seeing the family's needs as a collective, to viewing members' needs individually.

As attitudes have changed, there have been changes in the role that parents have been given within the parent-professional relationship. Some less active roles continue to be imposed on parents in certain specialty disciplines and by particular practitioners, while professional dominance remains a feature of many parent-professional working relationships.

Passive recipients of advice

Particularly in the early days, parents were expected to participate only passively in their children's educational or remedial programmes, accepting without question the advice of the professionals (Turnbull and Turnbull 1997).

Parents as learners

Many professional interventions are aimed at teaching parents specific skills for managing their child or for teaching their child skills which he or she is not learning naturally. However, some parents perceive this educational approach as patronizing, while Foster et al. (1981) claim that efforts to train parents are often redundant because many parents already have excellent skills for parenting and teaching their children.

Educational decision-makers

As professionals have increasingly given parents opportunities to do so, many parents have readily adopted the role of overseeing their child's education, calling schools to account for the curricula that they offer. Parental participation in planning educational programmes is legally mandated in the United States and Canada (Deslandes et al. 1999), and consequently is reflected strongly in the North American literature. In Australia and Britain, the involvement of parents in schools is encouraged at a policy – rather than a legislative – level, and so their participation differs across services and between practitioners.

Although today we anticipate that most parents will want to take an active part in decision making, some are content to leave the decisions to professionals, and so we must allow them to become involved at the level where they are comfortable. For some parents, the individualized education plan process is disempowering rather than empowering, as they find themselves facing a barrage of professionals and their advice, with the expectation that they will make a prudent decision based on incomplete understanding of the information that they are being told. Also, the formality of the meeting and the need to cover so much at once can unintentionally leave parents feeling discouraged.

Parents as teachers

In a shift away from blaming parents for their child's disabilities, many professionals instead gave parents the responsibility for remediation. They determined that parents were their children's 'first teachers' or 'best teachers', and thrust parents into the role of therapist or teacher of their children.

Whereas prior to this phase, parents' involvement might have been limited to attending case conferences only, or bringing the child in to treatment services, now parents were being asked to carry out some of the remedial strategies at home under the direction of professionals. This recognized parents' commitment and expertise and no doubt was motivated at least in part by the unavailability and high cost of more full-time professional services (Cunningham 1985), but this role imposed heavy responsibilities on parents. It placed many parents under enormous pressure to fulfil programme requirements, while ignoring their other duties and obligations to themselves, their partner, other children, and the child's emotional development.

Imposing equal responsibilities on parents confuses equality with sameness: professional and parental roles can be different while still having equal value. Parents function best as parents: they 'should not try to feel like teachers, or act like social workers or behave like psychologists'

(Blodgett 1971: 92). While some parents value a formal teaching role as it contributes to their own well-being and positive outlook (McKenzie 1996; Padeliadu 1998), other studies have found that the more time mothers spend in activities with their child, the more intense are their ratings of family problems (Harris and McHale 1989).

Furthermore, casting parents in the role of teachers fails to acknowledge the extensive informal teaching that parents already engage in continuously with their children, highlighting instead only formal instruction. Some parents do not want to play a formal teaching role, because it violates the uniquely personal component of the parent-child relationship (Seligman and Darling 1997), while other parents find it confronting to watch their child struggle with concepts and skills that came naturally to their siblings. It makes them sad for their child. And some children need very specialized interventions: given that sometimes their needs are beyond the skills of many professionals, it is safe to assume that they may also exceed the expertise of parents.

While parental involvement is seen to be crucial to the success of intervention programmes – especially in the younger years – *how* the parents interact with their child is seen to be more important than *what* they teach the child. This has led to relationship-focused interventions, where the aims are to enhance parent-child relationships by improving their communication. Thus, increasingly the emphasis is on teaching parents to recognize the communicative behaviours of their infants with disabilities, as atypical behaviours may be difficult for their parents to read and interpret (Yoder 1987). For instance, a blind child will not look towards parents in a bid for attention; a child with a physical disability might not snuggle in when cuddled. In contrast, then, to teaching parents specific content to pass on to their child, it has been shown to be more beneficial to teach parents to recognize the atypical cues that their child uses to communicate with them (Guralnick 1991). Parents who can learn to notice their child's alternative cues will then be able to respond to their child's bids for affection, which is the basis for a secure attachment to parents and, in turn, for further learning. Divesting parents of the responsibility for teaching their child while helping parents to identify these atypical social cues enhances the child's learning and parental satisfaction to a greater extent than does the parent acting as a teacher.

Parent advocates

By the beginning of the 1950s, many parents were beginning to get active and establish organizations to advocate for their children with disabilities. In response to a lack of services for their children and a lack of emotional support for themselves, many parents were instrumental in creating and developing services for people with disabilities and setting standards of care in institutions and community services.

Turnbull and Turnbull (1997) report that most members of these groups are still middle-class, white parents, and so parents' self-help and advocacy groups are not useful supports for all parents. Furthermore, the time and energy required both to coordinate and secure services for children is perceived by some parents as a drain on resources (McKenzie 1996; Turnbull and Ruef 1996). For example, in my study (Susan), mothers described having to be an 'advocate or carer, rather than a mother', and that 'fighting' for services, 'getting the run around' and 'dealing with the system' were as difficult (McKenzie 1996). Turnbull and Ruef (1996: 291) found, similarly, that parents resented 'the need to engage in extensive advocacy to hold professionals accountable for providing mediocre services'. Dealing with professionals and securing services for children clearly remains problematic for parents and profoundly affects the experience of parenting their child with special needs.

Conclusion on former roles of parents

As can be seen from the above discussion, parents can perform a number of roles with respect to their child's education or remedial programme. At one time, they were expected to be passive recipients of professionals' decisions, which gave them only one option. Subsequently, they were expected to become actively involved in their child's education. Again, only one option. Increasingly, it has become clear that, for a range of reasons, some parents do not want an active role. They might not feel equipped to make the decisions they are called on to make; they might be overwhelmed with other family issues; they might be sensitive to the need to balance the one child's needs with the needs of all other family members.

The theme in this text is that it is not up to professionals to decide for parents how they want to be involved, but it is our duty to listen to their wishes and facilitate the level of participation that they seek. Imposing roles on parents that assume a large amount of parental commitment – especially in the implementation of home-based programmes – can result in either guilt in parents, or criticism from professionals when parents are unable to fulfil unrealistic programme requirements (Foster et al. 1981). Professionals are like sprinters whereas parents are on a marathon, (Turnbull and Turnbull, 1997), and so do not need to be placed under pressure to be intensely involved in their child's education, as they may burn out and not be able to sustain their involvement throughout their son's or daughter's life.

The next phase: parents as employers

The collaborative perspective upholds that professionals and parents are full and equal partners. We do not believe this: in our view, this gives too much power to the professionals. As we see it, parents are employing professionals to offer a service to their child and so, clearly, the parents are in charge of our relationship with them. Parents consult us for our knowledge and experience of children with disabilities and employ us to support them in advancing their child's educational or other needs. More than being mere consumers or even equal participants in a partnership with you, parents are actually your employers. They pay considerable taxes for schools and other service agencies, and high fees for private services – and so, as to all employers, you are directly accountable to them for your practices.

Parents, then, are in charge of steering the services that their child requires. They remain in charge of exercising choice, accepting the consequences of their decisions, and planning for the realization of their long-term goals for their son or daughter. In order to achieve this, they need to recognize that they have something valuable to contribute (Bennett et al. 1998). Some will already be confident about their skills; others will have been deflated by personal experience, some of which may be with an impersonal or unresponsive service system, and subsequently they will lack confidence. Thus, as already mentioned, your job is not so much to empower parents, as to make sure that you do not disempower them. To ensure this, families need:

- recognition of their skills;
- encouragement to contribute to their child's education and to decision making;
- information about their options;
- a sense of control over their options;
- time and other resources, such as energy (Turnbull and Turnbull 1997).

All these requirements rest on the parents remaining in charge of their own lives, their own family, and their relationships with their professional advisers. One model that we find useful when thinking about the parents' need for self-determination is family systems theory. One branch of systems theory, the structural model, believes that every system or group arranges itself hierarchically. In a family, the parent or parents are executives and need to be able to function as family leaders. It might be useful to think of the parents as the hub of the wheel, from which all other relationships emanate. They are central to the family and must have power to exercise leadership over all aspects of family life.

The addition of a powerful person into the family – such as a professional adviser or a family member in crisis – can unbalance the family hierarchy and interfere with the parents' ability to function as its leaders. This concept places the onus on professionals who are working with parents whose child has a disability, to ensure that the parents can remain in control of any intervention and are not undermined by professional involvement.

This requires us to offer parents choices, and to give them accurate and up-to-date information so that they can make informed decisions about their options. Not only must this information be of high quality, but it also needs to be easily accessible to parents. We may also have to help parents to identify, understand and coordinate various sources of information.

When parents are not undermined in their role as family leaders, they are likely to have a personal belief in their own ability to plan, select and enact their choices for their child's services. In turn, this sense of self-efficacy will encourage them to participate in decision-making and in their children's schooling or other service (Deslandes et al. 1999). In short, parents who believe that they can be self-determining will harness the family's internal resources and will also be able to capture support from outside the family as required (Thompson et al. 1997). As well as improving the outcomes for their child, parents' sense of self-control is likely to lead to improved satisfaction with their relationship with their advising professionals (Turnbull and Turnbull 1997).

One aspect of the parent-professional relationship that can unwittingly undermine parents is the professional's attitude of helpfulness. The assumption that parents need professional help (by virtue of having a child who does) can lead to forms of helping that actually usurp the parents' control, disrupting their present skills and undermining their role as leaders and decision-makers in their family. This will be so if your help:

- increases parents' dependency on you and other professionals;
- lowers their self-confidence and sense of self-control;
- treats them as inadequate in some way;
- expects parent to feel indebted or grateful;
- supplies help in areas that the parents do not nominate or at times when they are not seeking help – that is, it 'rescues' parents and thus gives them the message that they are not competent at running their own lives (Dunst et al. 1988).

Placing parents in charge of their working relationship with professionals also has implications for family assessment. In the early days of working with parents, professionals were the ones to assess parents' 'needs' – which roughly translated into assessing their 'deficiencies' – and then workers set about correcting these. In the next phase, professionals were advised to focus instead on parents' strengths and harness those in the child's interests. In line, however, with the theme already developed in this chapter and expanded on throughout this text, we believe that it is not up to us to assess parents: it is our job only to listen to their statements about their own needs, and to respond to those.

This means that in assessment as elsewhere, parents are directing the flow. We do not assess them: they employ us to enact what they have assessed to be their own goals or aspirations for their child. Just like the child-centred perspective in which most of us were trained, the family-centred perspective relies on observation of and listening to individuals' needs and awareness of their interests and skills. Our main role, then, is listening, rather than talking or telling. It will also involve making available to families the options that they indicate they want (Hughes and May 1988). (This concept is expanded in Chapter 6).

In argument against this parents-as-employers or demand-based model of service delivery, Dale (1996) states that some parents do not know what they need, and so professionals should be making this assessment. We disagree. We can determine what services we can offer parents but we must give them the choice of whether to avail themselves of those services. If professionals try to impose on parents services that the parents do not want, they will resist anyway and the service will be ineffective. Instead, if we assume that all parents have more skills than they are using, it will be possible to expand their repertoire, as long as they have the support for doing so.

We recognize that sometimes it can be difficult to reconcile parents' wishes with what we assess to be in the best interests of their child (Hughes and May 1988) and that, in such situations, we must do what we can to advocate for children. But if we are not willing to listen to parents, they will not be willing to listen to our recommendations.

Thus, it is not just a matter of whether you meet families' needs, but of *how* you do so, so that parents can feel more rather than less confident as a result of how you work with them.

Constraints on collaborative relationships with parents

If families are not managing to solve their problems, this may have nothing to do with their personal lack of problem-solving skills, but may be due to a lack of resources and support for making decisions (Dunst et al. 1988, 1994). As a result, they may feel disempowered. Similarly, professionals can be disempowered if they feel that their role is not valued or that they do not have the resources that they need in order to provide high-quality services to children and their families. Not least of these resources is professionals' initial training, which seldom prepares them for working collaboratively with parents (McKim 1993). The outcome, when either parents or professionals lack resources or support, is that it becomes more difficult to work together collaboratively.

A second limitation is, of course, the parents' availability and resources for participating actively in their child's programme. However, as we have said already, intense participation is not necessary. Collaboration is a frame of mind which guides the way we work, rather than a level of participation.

A third impediment is that professionals are frequently judgemental of parents (Tinworth 1994). This may come about because we tend to work most closely with parents at their most stressful times, when there are problems. The result is that parents can seem to be less competent than they actually are. In addition, there are parents whose skills *are* difficult to respect. However, respect does not mean having to agree with parents; it simply means recognizing their values and perspective (Caughey 1991).

A fourth impediment is that parents and professionals can be keen to convey the 'right' impression to each other (Seligman and Darling 1997). In terms of your own 'impression management', it can help to remember that being professional does not mean having to be formal and distant with parents. They mainly want an emotionally rich relationship with the professionals with whom they deal, rather than a formal 'expert-client' relationship (Summers et al. 1990). Therefore although you are not ordinarily parents' friends – because being paid to deliver a service is not friendship – you can still be friendly.

Given these constraints, the most compelling feature of a collaborative relationship with parents is that it does not require us to learn new skills. It simply involves adjusting our notions of professional service. Instead of being a service that is given *to* others, we can see it as something that we do *with* them.

Summary

Over time, parents have become more empowered in their relationships with professionals. In this chapter we have argued for a further shift in power away from professionals towards parents, whereby the parents remain in charge of the working relationship and determine the services that their children receive. This shift in power can be uncomfortable because it will enable parents to question professional practice. However, as consumers of an expensive and important service, parents would be irresponsible if they did not closely question what you offer their child (Greenman and Stonehouse 1997). They both *need* and have a *right* to ask questions of the professionals who are working with them.

This version of collaboration does not imply any predetermined level of involvement of parents in their child's day-to-day programme, however. Programmes that impose active roles on parents can add to the parents' workload, increase their guilt if they do not carry out the programme exactly as directed, and may give parents the message that they are not allowed to respond emotionally to their child's disability, but instead must become very task-focused: 'Don't worry about that, just get on with this'.

Although clearly the early passive roles were disrespectful of parents, the adoption by many parents of more active roles came at considerable cost to them and other family members. Aware of these emotional costs, some parents choose to adopt a less active role. Although we might question this choice, we must support the parents' decision to safeguard the rights of all family members, not just the child who has the disability.

Not only must we allow parents to determine the *type* of role they will adopt in their child's programme, we must also allow them to determine how *intensively* they become involved. Pressure to participate at a level that is beyond the parents could inadvertently add to the stresses which they already experience in balancing the complex demands of their parenting and other roles (Sebastian 1989) and can detract from their quality of life (McKenzie 1996). Furthermore, we must give the family permission to *vary* their level of involvement in their child's programme over time, in response to fluctuating needs of themselves and other family members as their circumstances change.

Discussion questions

1. In your particular work situation, which form have relationships between the professionals and parents usually assumed? Why is that so?
2. What, in your view, is the significance of shifting from assessing parents' needs to listening to their aspirations for their child?
3. In your work setting, are there any constraints on working towards parents' goals for their child, rather than having professionals in charge of determining service priorities?

Chapter 2
The complexity of
family life

Programs that have been most successful in improving children's outcomes have taken the broad view of children's needs, viewing them within the context of their families . . . We are reminded of the African proverb: 'It takes a whole village to raise a child'.

Hanson and Carta (1995: 209–210)

Key points

- Sometimes, a moralistic or idealized view of the nuclear family causes us to believe that other family forms are less equipped to raise children successfully.
- When we communicate this view to parents whose families differ from the nuclear type, we disrespect them and detract from our ability to work with them.
- All families experience internal demands, some of which are generic and some of which relate to their family structure. Some also face additional challenges which tax their resources. This suggests that all families – whatever their form – can benefit from support from the wider community.

The family's social context

Just as children develop within the context of their family, so their family functions within a context of supports and strains introduced by the wider community. As depicted in Figure 2.1, these influences are arranged in layers or concentric circles, of which the relationships between the child and immediate family form the centre. At the closest level of influence are the child's and family's interactions with extended family members, friends, neighbours, caregivers, teachers and service professionals. At the next layer are local and state agencies that do not themselves comprise the child or family but relate with them from outside. This includes such structures as schools, child care services, churches, community groups, welfare agencies and health care systems. Finally, political, cultural, legal and community regulations and ideologies comprise the outermost layer and provide the context within which all the prior levels function.

Changes in any of these layers will reverberate through the family (Bronfenbrenner 1977). With this multi-layer model in mind, in this chapter we will examine both the internal features of the family that will affect its functioning, and then some external forces that will impinge upon it. Throughout, we will be relating these aspects to families whose child has a disability.

The concept of family

In order to collaborate with families, it can help to realize that the concept of *family* itself is changing. The Western notion of the family as being the nuclear group comprising married parents and their biological children is actually only about 50 years old and, almost as soon as it dominated our understanding of family life, became problematic because from the 1960s onwards, households across the Western world became more diverse (Gilding 1997).

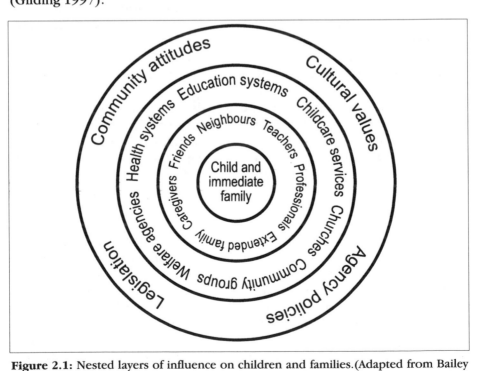

Figure 2.1: Nested layers of influence on children and families.(Adapted from Bailey and Wolery 1992: 66)

Meanwhile, our understanding of the function of families is shifting too. Over history, the family has been viewed as an economic unit with marriages arranged to advance the prosperity of the family and inheritances passed down from generation to generation; a subsequent view has been that the family's main function was to socialize children and to preserve the male-dominated social order, which implied that households could not function successfully without a male as their head; today, we tend to emphasize the family's nurturing and caring roles (Gilding 1997). This modern focus on nurturing has allowed us to regard a family as any 'two or more people who regard themselves as a family and who perform some of the functions that families typically perform' (Turnbull and Turnbull 1997: 11). In turn, this means that society will include homosexual couples within the definition of family, for instance, and speak of single-parent families as a variation in family form rather than as a failed, inferior or 'broken' family (Gilding 1997).

Some see these changes as unfortunate and maintain a nostalgic image of the 'traditional' family. There is a view that the family is the 'moral cell' (Gilding 1997: 45) of society and that departures from the nuclear structure are somehow immoral. Furthermore, this moralist view is coupled with the exaggeration of the impact of these changes on family life. This view is reflected in the language that is used about families, such as when we speak of 'intact' versus 'broken' families. When this moralist view is held by professionals who come into contact with parents, it can cloud professional-family relationships and service provision to families who do not conform to the idealized picture (Turnbull and Turnbull 1997).

If modern discourse is to be believed, the family is under siege from sudden changes in its composition. But there are two rebuttals to this notion. First, the things which are said to threaten the family – such as homosexuality and pre- and extra-marital sex – have always been a feature of life: they are probably no more prevalent now than they ever were, but we are talking about them more these days (Waters and Crook 1993). The majority of families remain nuclear, so the traditional family is not disappearing.

Second, the 'traditional' family is not always ideal. While most families support and nurture their members, some are sources of cruelty, violence and authoritarianism in the forms of child or spouse abuse (Waters and Crook 1993). In this chapter we will look at the changing structure of families, and then examine some of these less functional features of family life.

Family structure

The widespread community view about the demise of 'the family' tends to cause professionals to feel pessimistic about some families with whom they work, as it implies that some are less able to meet the needs of their members than can the traditional nuclear family. The following discussion exposes some of these myths, with the aim of reinstating professionals' confidence that all family types can function satisfactorily, as long as families have sufficient outside support for doing so.

Generational composition

The first myth is that families today lack the support of their extended family network because the generations no longer live together as they once did. However, the truth is that extended family members have never lived together – certainly not in Western cultures. Despite mythology, households in Britain have been stable in their membership and resulting size over the last 400 years (Bottomley 1983). Between 1574 and 1821, only 11% of British households included extended kin of any kind (Waters and Crook 1993). Thus, households have always been basically nuclear, although there are class differences in this picture (Gilding 1997). The portrait that we have of the extended family living together in the same household has come from the British landed gentry class, in which all family members had to remain on the family estate in order to maintain the property. Nevertheless, the limited average life span – especially in impoverished families – means that older generations were unlikely to be alive and so extended family households are not, in fact, part of our history.

Who is included in the household is culturally dependent. For example, within traditional Australian Aboriginal cultures it is more likely that grandparents and other extended family members will live with parents and children. On the other hand, many families will not conform to the pattern of their own particular culture.

When referring to families whose child has a disability, the lack of extended family as support is often cited as a difficulty for parents. However, despite our highly mobile societies, extended kin are probably now more available to the nuclear unit than they have ever been. First, increased longevity means that older generation members are still alive. Second, mass communication and fast transport mean that, where family members are not geographically close, nevertheless they can be emotionally supportive (Waters and Crook 1993). There is a distinction, then, between extended *households* – which, as we have just said, are now and have always been a minority – and extended *kinship*, which is now more available than ever, particularly in times of family crisis. This means that, as professionals, we do not need to assume that parents are parenting alone: grandparents may not live in the same location and may not be there to give practical help, but they can still give emotional support if family relationships are conducive.

Family size

Another myth is that families are much smaller now than they once were, thus depriving children of support from siblings. The number of children born to women in most Western countries today is hovering around two. But in Australia, this figure is the same now as it was a hundred years ago when, during the 1890s, around 20% of couples were not having children. Women born in the 1860s tended to have around five children with the result that the picture from 1880s suggests larger families, but subsequently fewer children became and remained the norm, as the figures in Table 2.1 illustrate.

Table 2.1: Number of births to cohorts of women

Women born	Number of children
1861–66	5.1
1903–08	2.6
1928–38	3.2
1940s	2.9
1960s	2.2

Sources: McDonald (1993); Waters and Crook (1993).

After 1900, birth control (in the form of condoms) became widely practised and the birth rate dropped from its previously high level. There was once again a slight rise in births to women born in the 1930s, which came about because they were marrying younger; the modern decrease in births comes about mainly because of the longer gap between marriage and the birth of the first child (Waters and Crook 1993). Nevertheless, the current birth rate resembles the rate for most of the last century, in which case it is not a significant change for the family.

Family size can affect the members' adjustment to a child's disability. A large family may cope better, as it will have more people to share chores, the parents have other children who respond to their parenting skills so their self-esteem is less at risk, and they may have some parenting experience if the child with the disability is preceded by older siblings. Other siblings can absorb parents' achievement expectations, rather than these being borne in small families by just one or two other children. Also, the child with a disability may seem more similar to than different from the other children in the family and so may be more readily accepted within the larger family. On the other hand, a smaller family may require fewer financial resources to meet its needs, and might be able to afford to buy in services that can reduce family members' workload.

Divorce

Divorce is a key feature of the modern family which is said to lead to the dissolution of individual families and, ultimately, will result in the demise of the family altogether. Taking each of these claims in turn, divorce dissolves *marriages*: it does not dissolve families. Second, despite the divorce rate, the two-parent family remains the dominant family type.

Just over half of Australian divorces are to couples with dependent children (Harrison 1993). The number of children whose parents divorce goes up by about 1% per year of the children's age, and so by the age of 18, 18% of all children will experience the divorce of their parents (Harrison 1993; McDonald 1993). We could rue these figures, but their converse is that over three-quarters of children live most of their childhood with both biological parents.

We must also acknowledge the positive side of the divorce laws that allow couples to leave their relationship when it is violent or unsupportive. Children growing up in these households experience more stress and disillusionment with relationships than children who grow up in sole-parent households where the parent is less stressed (Burns and Goodnow 1985). It is not being brought up in a 'broken' home that causes stress in children, but being brought up in a home in which there is conflict. Therefore, if a divorce ends conflict and does not result in poverty (as it often does), the children are better off than when living in a home where the parents are in conflict with each other.

Marriages are most at risk when the partners must fulfil the tasks of two life cycle stages at once (see Chapter 3). For instance, marrying under the age of 25 can mean that the partners have had insufficient time to disengage from their family of origin before establishing themselves as a couple; having a child at the time of marriage can mean that they have to learn to parent at the same time as establishing their couple relationship; marrying while still in education is a risk because education keeps students financially dependent, and so upon marriage they must master independent living at the same time as establishing their couple relationship.

Despite the divorce rates, marriages persist longer today than ever before. This somewhat surprising state of affairs comes about because spouses now live longer, as shown in Table 2.2. On its own, this table tells us little, but when we add the rate of divorce (1% at the beginning of the twentieth century) and informal separations (thought to be around 10% at the beginning of the twentieth century) to the death rates, then the percentage of Australian marriages that endure for 30 years is seen to be higher today than a hundred years ago. This is shown in Table 2.3.

So couples today are *more* likely to be living with their spouse after 30 years of marriage than has ever been the case. Whereas the death of one spouse once ended many marriages, today divorce severs marriages, but at a lower rate.

In a sample of 240 pre-industrial societies, only 18% were monogamous (which means marrying only one person at a time) (Waters and Crook 1993). The present divorce rate in Western countries does not indicate a decline in the importance of marriage, but a continued commitment to monogamy, albeit in a serial form.

There has long been the presumption that a child's disability increases the divorce rate for parents. The only figures pertaining to this issue are supplied by Fujiura (1998) for the United States. In that census study, the proportion of sole-parent households with a family member with a disability was double the usual rate – 40%, versus 20% for families without a member with a disability – with the majority of parents being separated, divorced or widowed; and just over a quarter never having been married. We cannot conclude, however, that this rate is universal, or that the cause of the higher rate of divorce is the child's disability as such: it may represent a coming together of many factors such as the parents' responses to the disability, the disruption to the family's life occasioned by professional involvement, and the lack of services and support provided to the family to counteract the additional demands that the disability may provoke.

Table 2.2: Percentage of marriages where both partners are still alive

	1891	1991
After 30 years	46%	88%
After 45 years	15%	56%

Source: McDonald (1993).

Table 2.3: Percentage of marriages where both partners are still alive and together

	1891	1991
After 30 years	41%	53%

Source: McDonald (1993).

Whatever the cause of a separation, while the divorce is occurring, individuals must contend with sometimes painful issues of grief for lost hopes and dreams about their family life. While they are in this process, they might be less available to meet additional demands such as contributing to their child's education or remedial programme. At the same time, the adults are likely to be parenting alone and so, even if emotionally available to participate, may have too little time to do so.

Sole-parent households

Another feature of family life that is thought to disadvantage children is sole-parent households. However, mother-headed households have been a significant feature of many societies and classes over time, including those societies in which the nuclear family has been idealized (Bottomley 1983). In the United States 28% to 34% of white children born between 1920 and 1960 lived with one or no biological parents; the figure for that period for African-Americans was 55% to 60% (Hanson and Carta 1995). This means that, historically, sole-parent households are not unusual.

The proportion of one-parent families with dependent children in Australia is reported in Table 2.4. In the USA in 1995, sole-parent households constituted just over one-quarter of all households (Mannis 1999). This figure and those in Table 2.4 tell us that sole-parent households are commonplace today but this was also the case a hundred years ago. They have also been prevalent in many periods during the intervening decades, as many fathers were away at the world wars or sought work away from home during the 1930s depression, sometimes not returning. The mothers who remained at home managed in those times to rear their children successfully; they can still do so today.

Becoming a parent at a young age can add to family stress, not least because poverty often accompanies young parenthood; in turn, family stress can negatively affect adolescents in particular (Murray-Harvey and Slee 1998). Nevertheless, sole mothers in Australia are decreasingly likely to be teenagers (McDonald 1993) and are unlikely to have chosen at the outset of their pregnancy to become single mothers to 'get social welfare benefits' as the myths would have us believe. Only 19% of single mothers

Table 2.4: Percentage of sole-parent families with dependent children

1991	16.6%
1974	9.2%
1891	16.7%

Source: McDonald (1993).

have not been married (Waters and Crook 1993). Most children who are now in sole-parent households were conceived within a long-standing relationship which dissolved after they were born: 29% of sole parents are separated; 35% divorced; and 14% widowed (Waters and Crook 1993). Having said this, some choose single parenting, with just over 20% of USA single mothers being in the age range of 30 to 44 years (Mannis 1999). These women are likelier to have more financial resources and social support for their parenting than teenage mothers, for instance.

The social problems that have been attached to single parenthood are not attributable to family dissolution itself or to children's growing up in single-parent households, but to the conflict that preceded the separation and which may be ongoing, and the poverty that often succeeds it. Sole-parent households are more likely to be in the lowest income bracket, to rent rather than own their accommodation, to live with another family so that they can share expenses, and to have limited access to private transport (McDonald 1993). However, sole parenthood does not of itself cause poverty: most families that are destitute after marital separation were poor prior to separation, but the separation can exacerbate their poor living circumstances. This comes about because, in uncontested custody cases, usually the woman receives the custody of the children. (The figure for contested cases slightly favours fathers, but such contests are few.) However, because the husband's education and work skills are likely to have progressed during the marriage while the wife's have stagnated, this means that the woman's income level following separation will frequently be lower than her former husband's.

Once again, the fact that sole parenthood has been characteristic of many families during many stages of our history suggests that sole parents have been and are capable of raising children successfully. Sole-parent families may be more similar to than different from dual-parent families. For instance, when it comes to sole parents of children with disabilities, the parents report similar issues to their married counterparts (Schilling et al. 1986).

Nevertheless, when we are working with sole parents, it will be useful to keep in mind that they are performing all of their family's child care and housekeeping roles on their own and so may have little time left over for additional responsibilities. (This awareness gives rise to Raines' [1995] observation that 'Single parents deserve double praise'.) Parenting children with disabilities may place additional demands on parents' time and stamina and can require a great deal of emotional energy. Given these many other demands, the more active parental roles in remedial services which we described in Chapter 1 may not be an option for these parents.

Step-families

The modern myth is that step-families are a new phenomenon, but remarriage rates are the same now as in the sixteenth and seventeenth centuries (Whelan and Kelly 1986). Instead of following the death of a parent, however, remarriage now typically follows divorce. This difference in the reason for remarriage signals the first difference between modern and earlier step-families – namely, that the grief process may differ. Children might regard their parents' separation as optional and so may find separation more difficult to adjust to than the death of a parent, which most will recognize as being unavoidable.

Second, although step-families were common some centuries ago, they have been less prevalent in recent history and so present-day step-parents do not have role models for how their families could or should function. They might try to model themselves on the nuclear family, using terms such as 'blended' families in an attempt to pretend that the differences in family of origin of the children do not matter, as fantasized in the perfection of the *Brady Bunch* or *The Sound of Music*. Or, they might feel stigmatized by folk lore about step-families as evidenced in fairy tales such as *Cinderella* and *Hansel and Gretel*. Neither role model is satisfactory and instead these families will need to find their own unique way of being a different type of family, without feeling deficient.

In Australia, subsequent to the introduction of the no-fault divorce laws in the mid-1970s (Family Law Act, 1975) there was a sudden peak in divorce and high rates of remarriage; now, remarriage rates are halved (McDonald 1993). Rather than marrying formally again, many divorcees who find a new partner instead live together or conduct their relationship from separate households. The latter is especially likely for women as they are most likely to have their children living with them.

As with sole parents, when working with a newly formed step-family, it would be a mistake to assume that it is like any biological family, dealing with the usual challenges of the life stage suggested by the ages of the children. The fact that the *marriage* is new (despite the children no longer being young) determines the demands on the family. Step-parents are performing many roles at once, with responsibilities spread across their present and former families, and are negotiating complex relationships among all family members. Furthermore, the family's grief from the dissolution of the previous marriage might not have been resolved, either for the adults or the children. Ongoing contact with the non-custodial parent can revive these feelings with each access visit.

Even when they are willing, therefore, to contribute actively to their child's programme, it may not be possible for them to devote the time and energy to it that they might wish.

Dual-income households

Yet another supposedly new challenge for modern families is the dual-income household. Some social commentators rue the fact that some families choose for both parents to work outside of home; others despair that some families are compelled to do so by the cost of living. It is assumed in both instances that the family is stressed by its workload. However, this argument assumes that all jobs are the same (Galinsky 1989), whereas if the parents feel satisfied with their work, they will have a better relationship with their children than if they find their jobs unfulfilling.

Second, it is likely that the pressures a family faces from the extra workload are more keenly felt in the family who is under financial stress than in the family who chooses to take on the additional commitments. On the other hand, when children are neglected as a result of their parents' working hours, they more readily adjust if they regard the work as a financial necessity than if they see it as an indulgence of their parents.

In 1954, only 13% of married women were in the paid work force; by 1986 this figure had climbed to 57%, with 40% of children aged under five having mothers in paid employment.

However, this is historically no different from the times prior to the turn of the twentieth century. At that time, industrialization had meant that a smaller labour force could produce all the required goods, in which case children were no longer needed in the labour market. At the same time, there were calls for a more skilled labour force and so universal education was introduced. Meanwhile, the men's wages increased such that it became possible to support families with just one wage. All these trends meant that both children and women were removed from the work place and women became responsible for child rearing (Grimshaw 1983). For the first time, women were defined as the moral leaders of the family without whom the family as an institution was said to be in jeopardy. The social expectation and norm thus became mothers who did not work outside of the home.

Even so, women from poorer backgrounds *never* had the choice between domestic and non-domestic labour: they have always had to do both (Bottomley 1983), while women of all classes in Australia participated at high rates in the work force during war years and times of economic depression. The only times in the twentieth century when women were less active in the work force were in the decade following World War I and preceding the Great Depression (1919–29), and the decade following the demobilization of troops after World War Two (1949–60). But in all other times, and particularly from the 1960s onwards, large numbers of women have worked outside of home.

So, our concept of mothers remaining at home is a very recent one, and has not been the norm except for a few brief periods during the twentieth century. Despite this recency, we have generated the syndrome of 'working mothers' on which we have blamed many current social ills.

Many professionals disapprove of working mothers, especially during the children's early years (Galinsky 1990). Such an attitude will impair their relationship with working mothers and has no basis in history or in fact. For instance, when the evidence is examined, it eventuates that mothers' participation in the work force during their children's early years is beneficial for the children's development, especially for those families who are on a low income. This is because paid employment can assist the family in financing the costs of meeting the children's developmental needs (Harvey 1999).

Working parents whose child has a disability often experience additional intrusions of their parenting role into their work setting, as appointments with specialists can be very frequent. Although they can ask for occasional time off work to deal with child-related issues, employers can be only so flexible. Thus, when both parents work, meetings between parents and professionals need to be held at times when the parents can attend (Berry and Hardman 1998; Bright and Wright 1986). We realize that it is not always possible to hold meetings out of hours: professionals have their own personal life and cannot commit all of their evenings to meetings. But it may be possible to avoid scheduling meetings at times when fathers can never attend, when transport is difficult, or when the parents cannot obtain a babysitter and so cannot both attend meetings.

Institutionalized child care

Women's desire to gain fulfilment from other than domestic duties places many in conflict between their work needs and their child-rearing commitments. The child care movement is growing in order to support parents who are managing both roles. Today, around half of Australia's children who are under five years of age attend child care, with around 23% attending professional care, half of which is delivered in child care centres (Butterworth 1991; Child Care Task Force 1996).

The need for child care is three-fold. The first is women's need for outside fulfilment, which many (especially in the middle classes) support. The second need is to support the child carer in the caregiving role, in the absence of other less formal supports. Modern western cultures are the first societies in which women have been the sole care providers for their children (Leach 1994). For many, sole child-rearing is too great a burden and so, in the absence of other support, some mothers turn to paid child care while the children are at a young age, or become stressed themselves.

The third need comes from the children themselves. It is now acknowl-edged that home-based care is less than ideal in some circumstances and at some ages (Tyler and Dettmann 1980), in which case a child's secure attachment to a caregiver or teacher can overcome a difficult home environment (Mitchell-Copeland et al. 1997).

Indeed, the bulk of research into high-quality child care centres has found that attending children show cognitive advances, are more sociable, have higher self-esteem, are more assertive, less likely to initiate conflict with peers, and are less aggressive than children with little or no centre-based care experience (Andersson 1989, 1992; Field 1991; Field et al. 1988; Howes 1990; O'Brien et al. 1999; Schwarz et al. 1973; Vandell et al. 1988).

These results on the developmental benefits of child care suggest that it is impossible for women to supply all of a child's educational needs, especially when families are struggling in their child-rearing role. This is especially crucial in a mobile society such as Australia's where extended family members may live elsewhere and so cannot give practical help.

Conclusion: The structure of the family

The nuclear family is often seen to be the 'proper' way in which to raise children. However, the above discussion tells us that modern departures from this family type are not very different from in the past. Despite apparent changes in its structure, in fact on most dimensions the modern family differs little from in the past. Thus, the family is not in decline as is sometimes assumed. Furthermore, as previous generations have not suffered noticeably from variations to the nuclear family, we can assume that current generations will similarly thrive within their particular family type.

Children grow up accepting whatever family type in which they are reared. Indeed, says Bottomley (1983: 12), 'this is how cultures are trans-mitted.' Given that children can function well whatever their family setting, it makes no sense to talk about certain family structures as 'deviant'. This enlarged perspective on families allows us to deem all family types – be they step-families, sole-parent families, or families from other cultures – as valid family forms. This acceptance will allow us to work with all parents and children respectfully and with the optimism that they can, with appropriate support, meet the needs of all their members. On the other hand, it is clear that some families face additional challenges which arise from both internal and external circumstances.

Additional challenges for families

Aside from the unique challenges posed to families by their structure, some face additional challenges from circumstances such as poverty and drug use. When these are part of family life, they can undermine the parents' self-confidence and sense of control over their own lives (Hanson and Carta 1995). Being outside the dominant culture can also restrict the parents' access to services and community supports.

Poverty

Germaine Greer (1999) speaks of the feminization of poverty on the grounds that it is usually the female parent who is left raising the children on her own. This, however, signifies that poverty accompanies children, who are the most disadvantaged by it.

Any family structure can overcome all stressors – except poverty. This, then, is the single most important external stressor on families. While it would be misleading to say that all impoverished families dysfunction as a result of their poverty, it is fair to say that their limited financial resources and limited external support place a strain on their internal support mechanisms.

In Australia, poverty is a relative concept: few people experience actual starvation, but many children (21%, or 800,000) live in relative poverty, without sufficient income to cover living expenses, health and educational costs. This figure is a change from 1970, when it was estimated that 8% of children lived in poverty, and is higher than for other Western cultures, with the exception of the US (Gilding 1997).

There are various ways of classifying poverty: according to a proportion of the average wage, as defined by the unemployment benefit; or as defined in indices such as given in Table 2.5. In addition to absolute measures of family income, a further issue is the *duration* of poverty: a family with a recently unemployed head may temporarily meet the deprivation criteria, although its standard of housing, for example, may be quite high, given that until recently it received a regular income. On the other hand, a family whose adults have been unemployed in the long term, despite presently being on the same income as the first family, may have considerably poorer living standards.

Whichever measure of poverty is used, it is clear that being from a non-dominant cultural group or having English as one's second language, puts one at far greater risk of living in poverty. In turn, such families are at greater risk of disability, caused by poor nutrition, poor prenatal care, and young parenthood (Hanson and Carta 1995; Seligman and Darling 1997).

Although impoverished families share similar values to the dominant groups in their society, they realize that they cannot access the goods and services that are available to others. Families who are experiencing poverty face multiple challenges which make it more difficult for them to respond to a child's special needs or be actively involved with disability profes-

Table 2.5: Typical indicators of poverty

Component	Typical indicators
Health and the availability of medical aid	Ability to walk 100 metres without difficulty, to walk stairs and to run 100 metres, feeling of tiredness during last week, various symptoms of pain and illness
Employment and working conditions	Unemployment during the last year, noise and temperature in workplace, monotonous physical work routine
Economic pressures and consumer protection	Income and wealth, ability to come up with £400 within a week
Knowledge and education	Years of formal education, level of education received
Family and social relations	Marital status, visits to relatives and friends
Housing	Number of household members per room, housing amenities
Recreation pursuits	Vacation trips, leisure time
Security of life and property	Victimisation through violence, damages and theft
Political resources	Voting in elections, membership in parties and unions, participation in the public debate, ability to file formal complaints

Source: Erikson and Uusitalo (1987, in Brownlee 1990: 33).

sionals, as they may already be engaged with the social welfare sector on more basic issues (Simpson 1990: 16–17).

Professionals tend to come from the middle classes, whereas parents come from all socioeconomic levels. As a result the two may have highly divergent views about disability and its treatment, which need to be resolved for them to work together collaboratively (Seligman and Darling 1997). Parents who are living in poverty may experience the scrutiny of social welfare agencies, with the result that many keep their problems to themselves for fear of activating social policing measures (Gilding 1997).

Parents who have a disability are more likely to be living in poverty, as will be seen in the discussion in Chapter 6. Parents whose children have disabilities may have restricted incomes as one parent (usually the mother) reduces her working hours so that she can meet the child's additional needs (Barnett and Boyce 1995) and, at the same time, the family has additional expenses to meet. Although this issue is addressed in Chapter 3, it is worth saying here that professionals must be aware of the restrictions that low incomes can place on parents, and on the parents' need to balance their spending on the child's care with other calls on the family purse.

Membership of non-dominant cultures

In modern multicultural societies, it is inevitable that professionals will come into contact with children and families whose culture imbues them with a variety of value systems (Simpson 1990). Nevertheless, it is important not to stereotype families on the basis of their cultural or class membership, as individuals will vary as greatly within those groups as individuals do within the dominant cultural group.

Various cultures favour cooperation over individual endeavour, and so achievement of the person with a disability may be less important to families from such cultures than the wellbeing of the family as a whole. Other families might not be as future-focused as is common in Western cultures, and may be more concerned with present issues. As a result, their goals for their adolescent son or daughter might differ from the dominant culture's view. For instance, they might not seek independence training for their child in the belief that children should leave the parental household only when they marry – and they do not expect their son or daughter who has a disability to marry. A second example is that some parents might not expect their son to contribute to housekeeping and so they object to such training for him.

Whatever their cultural expectations and beliefs about disability, those who are from the non-dominant cultures may lack wider social support for their cultural way of life. They may lack facility with English to access services they require; they may not turn to outside support, expecting that their family will support itself if that has been their cultural practice; or they could lack faith in the wider community, so that they avoid even enquiring into services.

When working with migrants, it is helpful to bear in mind that they will have received their education in their homeland and so are likely to feel nervous of their understanding of the schooling system in their new country. Their home country might emphasize professional dominance, which will be reinforced by their devalued status as migrants and lack of facility with the dominant language – particularly with specialist terms as found in the disability field. This means that you will have to be sensitive to those who are reticent about working collaboratively with you and encourage whatever steps they make toward that goal.

Child abuse

The cherished nuclear family has always had its shortcomings: a large minority of families fail to nurture their members, while some actively harm them through child or spouse abuse. Child abuse is one of those phenomena that has probably been present at similar rates for as long as the family has existed. However, today we are talking about it more. Child abuse takes a number of forms:

- neglect of children's physical or emotional needs;
- physical abuse;
- emotional abuse;
- sexual abuse.

We know that most child abuse occurs at home, that most abusers are known to the child and that up to 40% of children are sexually or physically abused, with half of the sexual abuse beginning during the preschool years.

Bottomley (1983) contends that caring for children without help is too much for a large minority of families, whose stress is expressed in physical and verbal abuse. When children are non-disabled, child maltreatment is an indicator of the overall quality of life for families (Garbarino and Gilliam 1980). Child abuse is more common and less easily detected in families that are socially isolated, suggesting that these families and children lack sufficient support from the community. This means that in searching for causes, we must look beyond the immediate family to the community that permits child maltreatment and fails to offer parents the necessary support in their childrearing role. If this picture is correct, the way to prevent child abuse is to reduce the stress that parents are under.

The second conclusion from the child abuse statistics is that if we can prevent abuse in the home, then the main source of abuse is removed, and children will not grow up expecting to be abused outside of the home. Ways to prevent child abuse in the home include wide dissemination of alternative methods of parenting to the power-based approaches of praise and punishment, and to ensure that siblings (a significant source of child abuse) are not permitted to bully each other within the family and thus achieve the greater psychological strength that allows them to perpetrate abuse.

A recent phenomenon to affect child abuse is substance abuse. Parents' intoxication can lead to neglect of children. The use of illicit drugs occurs across all sectors of the community but it is likely to have most impact on those families who are already impoverished (Hanson and Carta 1995). Prenatal exposure can lead to developmental disabilities in children, such as foetal alcohol syndrome, whose prevalence is rising concomitantly with the increase in drinking by young women.

Abuse of children with disabilities

People with disabilities are around two-and-a-half times more likely to be physically or sexually abused than people without disabilities (Sobsey and Mansell 1997). Kurtz and Kurtz (1987) report that child abuse is both a response to and a cause of disabilities in children, severe cases of abuse and neglect producing delays in all areas of children's development.

As is the case for all populations, many of the perpetrators of abuse of people with disabilities are within the young person's intimate circle of friends and relatives; a significant proportion of abuse (14–33%) is perpetrated by professionals; and some perpetrators are intellectually disabled themselves.

Often, the reason for their increased vulnerability is assumed to be that children with disabilities are more difficult to parent, creating stress in their caregivers (although as we report in Chapter 4, this is not necessarily so). Two lines of research refute this assumption. First, abuse is no more common among more stressed parents than among less stressed parents; second, the prevalence of abuse by professionals – whose level of stress must be lower than that of full-time carers – suggests that stress cannot account for the phenomenon of abuse (McCartney and Campbell 1998; Sobsey and Mansell 1997). Furthermore, earlier beliefs that caregiver stress was the cause of the abuse came about from *asking the abusers*, who rationalized their actions by blaming their victims (Sobsey and Mansell 1997).

The hypothesis of increased stress as a causal factor in abuse appears to be supported by the fact that severity of disability – and, thus, high caretaking needs – is related to a higher incidence of abuse. However, Sobsey and Mansell (1997) argue cogently that this is because for high-dependency young people, there are more personal domains in which caregivers must intrude, and there is a greater imbalance of power between a caregiver and highly dependent young person. It is the imbalance of power – and the young person's inability to disclose the abuse – that is allowing the abuse to be perpetrated, not the high caretaking needs as such.

Professional intervention may exacerbate the vulnerability of young people with disabilities. The first avenue for this is behaviour modification programmes, whose goal is to train young people to do as directed. This may teach them not to question directives to participate in abuse. Second, as we saw in Chapter 1, placing parents in a teaching role can violate their natural caregiving functions, disrupting the emotional bond between parent and child and thus giving the child no one to whom to report abuse that is occurring elsewhere (Sobsey and Mansell 1997).

Some medical treatments and ongoing physical care routines can violate young people's privacy, making it more difficult for them to detect when this is not warranted. Furthermore, some instances of medical care are clearly inappropriate. For instance, Conway (1994) details cases of forced feeding, restraint, deprivation of food, and aversive therapy which were carried out in the name of remedial treatment. A second example comes from an occasion when I (Louise) had to clear out old case files of young people with disabilities. In these I found, among other items, naked photos taken of them as children by doctors, stapled to the front of their file. When I asked the medical practitioner in the agency what was the purpose of the photos, she said it was to help identify the children. She did not explain quite how a photo of a naked nine-year-old girl could help identify a clothed woman now 30 years old, however. Children who are accustomed to justifiable medical interventions might not have the same sense of privacy about their bodies as others: and if doctors can take naked photos of you, then what grounds would a child have for refusing others' requests for the same thing?

Last, we make young people vulnerable to sexual abuse when we do not teach them about their sexuality (Conway 1994; Sobsey and Mansell 1997). If they are ignorant, it can be easier to convince children with intellectual disabilities that sexual abuse in particular is everyday behaviour. They would then not realize that it should be reported. Their dependency on the goodwill and ethics of others, then, would be reduced if we taught them that they have a right to resist the imposition of control (in whatever form) by others, even caregivers; and encouraged their use of skills for resisting, such as assertiveness (Conway 1994).

Obstacles to reporting abuse

Most abuse goes unreported, partly because of the difficulties of detecting the abuse and partly because of the obstacles to reporting it (Conway 1994). Detection is difficult when families are isolated and the children's communication disabilities make it difficult for them to disclose the abuse. Even community-based living is no barrier against institutional abuse, as with fewer staff in attendance, it can be more difficult for caregivers to observe another caregiver's abuse of residents.

The politics in institutions and society in general present obstacles to reporting (Conway 1994). Moreover, children who are members of non-majority cultures are doubly precluded from reporting, as these children may be suspicious of authority (which is vested in the dominant cultural group) and will be reluctant to attract the attention of authorities to their family for fear of feeding racist myths and cultural stereotypes (Bernard

1999).

Teachers are in an ideal position to detect the signs that may signify abuse. On the basis of the saying that 'I wouldn't have seen it if I hadn't believed it', the first step is realization of the high rate of child abuse in society in general and the increased risk faced by children with disabilities. Awareness will allow you to look out for signs of abuse such as burns or bruises, children's sudden change of behaviour (coinciding with the onset of abuse), refusal to accompany a particular adult, generalized reluctance to hug any family member, developmental regression (such as bedwetting, soiling, or regressed language skills) and, for verbal children, frequent discussion about secrets or about sexual practices, knowledge of which is in advance of the children's years or developmental level.

In Australia, all paediatric practitioners are legally obliged to report suspicions of abuse and, although Freedom of Information legislation allows most details of clients' files to be disclosed to them, the identity of the reporter remains confidential. Therefore, teachers are safe to report their suspicions of abuse. Nevertheless, they often fail to do so, perhaps because they fear that they lack proof (Pearson 1996). However, it is the social welfare agency's job to gather proof and any unskilled attempts to collect this prior to a proper inquiry can cause a child to clam up and thus hinder future investigations. Instead, you should report your concerns, because although your information on its own may not be enough for authorities to go on, for all you know, a child's case may already be under investigation and so, combined with earlier reports, your information might allow the child finally to receive some protection (Pearson 1996).

Summary

When you put together the statistics presented in this chapter, you find a pattern of family life that is not so very different from the past and so need not give rise to forebodings of doom for the modern family. Nevertheless, the many family configurations where children now live cannot be treated as being identical: there are differences in the needs and support available within families, and hence differences in their requirements for external support. When families are experiencing multiple stressors, it is clear that no single intervention will be effective (Hanson and Carta 1995) but support must be provided on many fronts.

As we will be emphasizing in coming chapters, it is important not to blame a family's present difficulties on the presence of disability in the family. It could have nothing to do with the problem. Similarly, the family's structure might not be the cause of any problems that they are experiencing. However, it is clear that families that deviate from the nuclear model tend to be given less support and are subjected to additional scrutiny by the community, and this stigma may cause some difficulty for them. Thus, external pressures on them to conform may be the problem, not their own internal demands.

Discussion questions

1. What implications does family structure have for parents' availability to be involved in their children's education or other services?
2. In general, do you believe that the families in your service receive sufficient social support?
3. How does poverty affect the services that children and families require, and the ability of service providers to meet their needs?
4. What measures do you feel need to be enacted to protect children in your school or service from child abuse?

Chapter 3
Families across the life span

The needs and characteristics of families are not only varied but also in a state of constant change. Accordingly, parental and family involvement requires that professionals be familiar with the trends that impact on parents and families; the range of needs encountered by parents and families with exceptional members; methods for individualizing parent and family involvement; and strategies appropriate for serving their needs.

Simpson (1990: 34)

Key points

- Families have some functions that they must fulfil for as long as they are a unit.
- In addition, there are specific challenges that arise in response to the changing ages and developmental stages of the family members.
- The disability of a member of the family can affect both how the family fulfils its functions and how it negotiates the transitions from one life stage to the next.

Introduction

This chapter discusses how a family's involvement in their child's services will be affected by the other tasks that the family has to perform. At any one time, they must fulfil basic life-sustaining functions, upon the satisfaction of which they are able to attend to higher-order needs. As well as this, throughout time, the challenges that families face change with the ages and stage of development of their members.

At the outset of this discussion, it is worth noting that families where there is a child or children with disabilities are likely to be as ordinary as any other family (Behr and Murphy 1993). In the words of McCormack, the term 'ordinary', however, is not used:

in any condescending sense of being dull or uninteresting or greatly alike, but in being not much different from the people next door or the family down the road, who do not happen to have a [disabled] child.

McCormack (1978, cited by Hughes and May 1988: 95)

Family functions

Having looked at the factors that can impinge on families from the outside in Chapter 2, we will now turn to looking at how families function on the inside. Families have three functions:

1. Basic need satisfaction for members: food, shelter, safety, clothing;
2. Developmental adaptation and socialization of children;
3. Crisis management.

Abraham Maslow categorized individuals' needs in a hierarchy from the lower-order needs for survival, safety and protection, to the higher-order emotional needs. The same is true for families: if a family is struggling to meet its basic needs, it will find it more difficult to adjust to the additional requirements of having a child with a disability.

Thus, a successful intervention will balance the needs of all family members at any given time. Each family member is seen to have his or her own needs which are legitimate and must be satisfied – both in that person's own interest and in the interests of all members, including a child with a disability (Appleton and Minchom 1991; Turnbull 1988).

Economic functions of families

All families must maintain their financial viability, but many families have to operate within a context of financial hardship, and this can be exacerbated when a child has a disability (Bailey et al. 1992; McKenzie 1994; Rasmussen 1993). Lack of finance reverberates throughout the family as it limits members' activities and opportunities and is an ongoing source of stress for parents (Minnes 1988). If social security benefits exist, these can partially offset the costs of specialist treatments, although the cost of these can exceed any income supplements. Where the family must pay for services, this can lead to delays in obtaining services until the parents can afford them.

In Australia, structural adaptations to the home (such as ramps and handrails in bathrooms) can be organized through Domiciliary Care, although many alterations may not qualify for this service. Some parents might not know that there is such a service or that they would be eligible to receive it and so they do not ask and instead would pay for alterations themselves. Meanwhile, in Australia at least, much special equipment is subsidized by the health care system. However, there are other hidden costs which parents must bear themselves – such as the better-quality shoes recommended by a podiatrist which are more expensive than the usual shoes that parents would buy for a non-disabled child.

Thus, depending on the local social security schemes, families may or may not experience additional costs of providing for the special equipment needs of their children with disabilities. However, many experience a restriction on the family income as caretaking parents (usually mothers) find that they cannot return to the paid work force as they had been planning. Many find that the number of appointments and their level of involvement in their child's programme can make it difficult for them to return to work. Even when mothers do return to the work force, they tend to reduce their employment by seven hours a week (Barnett and Boyce 1995). This will restrict the family income considerably both at the time and perhaps permanently, as the mothers' restricted work opportunities result in loss of experience, reduced training opportunities and less likelihood of promotion to senior positions.

A final added expense is where respite care is unavailable through the public system, in which case baby-sitters must be paid for. Seligman and Darling (1997) report this to be the greatest single expense experienced by many families in a 1984 study by Harbaugh (in the USA).

When the person with the disability reaches adulthood, restricted employment opportunities and the consequent fact of the young adult's probable ongoing financial dependence on the family may affect the parents' retirement decisions.

Physical care functions

Caring for children is a second key function of families. All young children require a good deal of physical caretaking, which families generally can accommodate as these demands tend to reduce over time. However, as children with disabilities grow older, their caretaking needs do not reduce as much as is the case for children without disabilities. Their increased size can make caretaking more physically demanding for their parents (Alper et al. 1995) while those with an intellectual or learning disability may expose themselves to danger as they become more mobile but are unaware of the risks of their actions.

Such prolonged caretaking is a risk to the parents' relationship and to the wellbeing of individual family members, as they neglect their own needs in favour of the child's. To avoid adding to such pressures, any remedial programmes will need to emphasise teaching children self-care skills, at whatever level is achievable for them.

Recreation

A third function of families is to play together and to facilitate family members' recreation in the wider community. In my study, I (Susan) found that a significant proportion of parents who had preschool children with disabilities felt that their children's difficult behaviour made home life stressful and restricted the recreational activities of their families (McKenzie 1994). The children's behaviour made parents reluctant to leave the children in the care of friends, extended family members or child care services. The same finding for parents of girls with Rett syndrome was reported by Perry and colleagues (1992) where fathers in particular reported that they had few opportunities to meet their own needs and to engage in recreational activities; the same was found for mothers of children with developmental disabilities (Rasmussen 1993).

The following factors can make it more difficult for the family to satisfy its recreation needs, especially as a unit rather than individually:

• With a child in the family who has a disability, family outings can need extra organizing in advance, which may make these outings less attractive (McKenzie 1996).
• Public outings can lead to embarrassment for family members. Siblings might be more keenly embarrassed than the adults, given children's egocentric stage of development.
• The activity chosen to suit the disabled child's needs may not suit the other children, who as a result become reluctant to participate.
• Children with a disability may have extra difficulties entertaining themselves, and so might make more demands on the time which other family members would otherwise use for their own recreational purposes.

Parents are not only concerned about their own recreation needs. They also want their children to have opportunities to balance work with play, have some respite from scheduled activities, relax, cuddle and have fun rather than having to work always to advance developmentally (Coots 1998).

Socialization function

Families must also encourage their members to socialize with others outside of the family. Parents of children with intellectual or learning disabilities report that their child's special needs can cause them to have less time available for social activities. Barnett and Boyce (1995) found, for instance, that mothers lost three and fathers lost two hours per week in socialization time, although other researchers found no change for mothers and an increase in available time in the case of fathers (Rasmussen 1993).

Not only can the amount of time be restricted, but what members can do with their available time might also be curtailed, for the following reasons:

- A child with certain disabilities might have limited skills for socializing.
- The community may fear or reject the child or even the whole family, leaving them more isolated than they would otherwise be.
- The parents' socializing may be curtailed through losing friends (McKenzie 1996) and through finding it difficult to obtain a baby-sitter, as some people feel unequal to the special demands of caring for the child with the disability.
- The demands on parents to participate in their child's remedial programme can leave insufficient time for them to have a social life (Barnett and Boyce 1995).

Sometimes, a child's disability can increase parents' opportunities for socialization – for example, when they participate in parent support groups, or when they can locate respite care for their child with special needs, thus allowing other family members to have some time to socialize together without the child who has the disability. Meanwhile, even when their opportunities for socialization are restricted, many parents nevertheless are satisfied with the relationships they do have.

Affection function

Another function of families is the exchange of affection between family members. A child's disability can bring the family closer; on the other hand, it can create more distance between members. This can be exacerbated when the child's life span is expected to be short. As shared affection is one of the most important family functions, an intervention programme must ensure that it does not demand so much time of parents that it depletes the time available for the family to enjoy each other's company.

Self-identity function

Family membership plays an important role in helping individuals to establish who they are and recognize their worth as people. Parents of a child with a disability can have a crisis of self-confidence, feeling incompetent to satisfy the child's special needs. This can be alleviated when a programme includes activities that do not centre around the disability, and by offering parents choices. Being able to make decisions can offset the feelings of incompetence that some parents may experience.

Educational/vocational function

The final function of families, as listed by Turnbull and Turnbull (1997), is that families must help launch young people into the world of work and, in preparation for that, the world of school. Despite this being a high priority for most families, professionals often emphasise the academic side of education whereas parents generally place a higher priority on functional skills and social participation (Westling 1996). Therefore, in planning priorities for services, it is crucial to listen to parents' aspirations for their son or daughter, and to consider not only the child's overall development, but also the needs of the family as a whole.

The family life cycle

All families must fulfil the above functions. As well as that, through time, family members grow older and the tasks that the family performs change. This is termed a family 'life cycle'. The stages are reproduced in Table 3.1 and will now be described briefly.

Table 3.1: The stages of the family life cycle

Stage	Tasks
Unattached young adult	• Differentiation of self from family of origin • Development of intimate peer relationships • Establishment of self in work
Newly married couple	• Commitment to relationship • Realignment of relationships with extended family and friends to include spouse
Family with young children	• Adjusting marital relationship to make space for child/ren • One parent suspending outside work if home-based care is chosen • Assuming parenting roles • Realignment of relationships with extended family to include parenting and grandparenting roles
Family with adolescents	• Flexibility in parent-adolescent relationships to allow the young person increased independence • Refocus on mid-life marital and career issues • Increasing concerns for older generation
Launching children	• Renegotiation of marital system as a dyad • Acceptance of repeated entries and exits from family • Development of adult relationships with adult sons and daughters
Later life	• Dealing with declining personal health • Dealing with disability or demise of one's own parents • Dealing with the loss of spouse, friends, siblings • Preparation for one's own death

Source: adapted from Carter & McGoldrick (1980: 17).

Disengagement and commitment

The family life cycle begins with disengagement from one's family of origin. Unsuccessful disengagement at the time of marrying introduces a stressor on the new family, and is a significant cause of subsequent divorce.

Couples without and then with children

Whereas it was once thought that lives changed upon marriage, it appears that they do not change nearly as much then, as when children arrive. When first married, the spouses have roles that are flexible and interchangeable. The structure of the family without children allows for a wide variety of solutions to immediate problems. However, these interactional patterns and roles often change with the physical and emotional commitment to children.

Later life

Today, the majority of couples can expect their adolescents to leave home, and will have to realign their marriage accordingly. A hundred years ago, few parents experienced this stage of family life, because of their shorter life span, late childbearing, and because one child often remained at home because he or she did not marry. Today, when one parent (frequently the mother) feels abandoned, she is said to be experiencing 'empty nest' syndrome, in which there is little to replace her former parenting role. As young couples are having children later in life, there can be some considerable gap between the time when adolescents leave home and become parents themselves, and so the role of grandparent may not quickly replace the role of parent.

Exceptions to these stages

Many families are under stress because these life cycle stages do not succeed each other in an orderly progression and so they must master the tasks of two stages simultaneously. This is apparent, for instance, when a couple marry when one or both already have children from prior relationships and so have to establish their couple relationship at the same time as learning to parent the children. The discussion in Chapter 2, however, recognized that many families can cope with these challenges: the exceptions signify merely that, in the face of multiple demands, families may require additional support.

Family life cycle in a family whose child has a disability

As we have seen, families change as their members age, with each new developmental stage bringing its own challenges. When the family has a

child with a disability, additional challenges may be added at each stage of
the life cycle (Seligman and Darling 1997). Table 3.2 adapts Turnbull and
Turnbull's (1990) list of possible issues encountered through the life
stages in families where a child has a disability.

Table 3.2: Possible issues encountered at various life cycle stages by parents whose
child has a disability

Early childhood (0-6 years)
- Obtaining an accurate diagnosis
- Informing siblings and relatives about the child's disability and needs
- Locating services
- Seeking meaning in the exceptionality
- Clarifying a personal ideology to guide decisions
- Confronting social stigma
- Identifying positive contributions of the child's disability
- Setting high expectations
- Negotiating the involvement of professionals in the family
- Participating in early intervention services

Primary school age (6-12 years)
- Adjusting to loss of previous support personnel
- Establishing routines to carry out family functions
- Adjusting emotionally to implications of choice of school
- Adjusting to reduced communication with school personnel
- Locating community resources
- Arranging for extracurricular activities

Adolescence (ages 12-21 years)
- Adjusting emotionally to possible chronicity of the child's disability
- Dealing with issues of emerging sexuality
- Encouraging social contacts outside home
- Planning for employment and independent living beyond school

Adulthood (ages 21+)
- Planning for care for the adult in the event of their own death or
  incapacity
- Locating appropriate living arrangements for their son/daughter
- Encouraging social activities independent of the family
- Initiating employment
- Re-establishing a personal life for selves

A child's developmental delay can have four effects on the family life
cycle:

- It delays the child's personal developmental timetable as milestones take
  longer to achieve, if at all (depending on the severity of the disability).

- It can accelerate the personal life cycle of siblings as they take on responsibilities beyond their years.
- It can delay the family life cycle in line with the child's developmental delays; or it can hasten it as the parents come into contact with human services that they do not ordinarily access until later ages, if at all.
- It can isolate the family from others because caretaking demands can increase at times when they ordinarily reduce: compared with other families, this causes social asynchrony – that is, a sense of being out of step with others (Mallory 1996).

Obviously, however, there are many aspects to family life other than one member's disability. This means that how families respond will be affected by the other simultaneous demands that their present stage of development requires them to meet and the accessibility of suitable support services (Llewellyn et al. 1999a, 1999b).

Encountering the disability

The normal life cycle can be disrupted for the first time when the family becomes aware of their child's disability. This can precipitate a crisis affecting the whole family, perhaps immobilizing it for a time as members devote their energies to dealing with the powerful emotions that they are experiencing. More so than at any other stage of their child's life, parents in the early weeks of adjusting seem to pose questions about their child's long-term prospects and can ask existential questions about the meaning of it all for them and their child; only later do they adopt the approach of taking it one day at a time (Hughes and May 1988).

The parent-child relationship can be disrupted by the manner of discovery of the child's disability, and by having the child's care 'taken over' by the experts. Sensitive professional involvement can avoid these risks. Sometimes, the parents have actually been concerned for some time about their child's development and so an eventual diagnosis can be met with some relief; in other instances, the child's disability might have been diagnosed soon after birth or might have been acquired later through an illness or accident, in which case shock is likely to be the first reaction.

Not only do the parents encounter the child's disability but so too do other family members. Sometimes, managing the reactions of those around them is more stressful for parents than managing their own responses (Hayes 1998).

Early childhood

It is often during the early childhood years that a child's disability is discovered and the family first becomes involved with professionals. Or, if the parents have been aware since birth of their child's special needs, it is often during the early childhood years that the chronicity of the child's disability can become clearer to the family. They realise – perhaps for the first time – that their child is not achieving and will not achieve developmental milestones at the usual age, a fear which can be reinforced by their contact with older children who share their child's disability.

It is also during these pre-school years that parents become aware of the services needed by their child, and the demands that these can place on their time, energies, and finances. Although the parents' intense involvement with their young child can seem quite natural at first, this high degree of involvement can be prolonged when their child has special needs, sometimes to the detriment of other family members. For example, when parents feel that services for their child are inadequate, they may unintentionally neglect the needs of other family members in their fight to secure the services that they believe their child requires.

Just as parents are becoming involved with professionals, these early years of a child's life often signal the beginning of professionals' long-term contact with the family, with its positive and negative impacts on all areas of family functioning. For instance, professionals can unwittingly add to parents' stress by pressuring them to be their child's teacher or therapist.

School entry

While the early intervention programme was intended to ameliorate the child's disability, the choice of school brings awareness painfully home to parents that it has not done so and, indeed, never could have. If the parents have been actively involved in the delivery of remedial programmes, they can feel cheated and disillusioned that they gave up so much to achieve so little of what they had hoped.

Like all parents, those whose child has a disability are excited at the prospect that their child will start school, but it is also a stressful time (Bentley-Williams and Butterfield 1996). They have to leave familiar programmes and staff and accept that, at school, there is generally less opportunity for their involvement (Bentley-Williams and Butterfield 1996; Hadden and Fowler 1997). Many are concerned that the school may not be receptive to the information they wish to impart about their child's history and present needs, and are concerned for their child's safety in the more loosely supervised school playground (Bentley-Williams and Butterfield 1996). Moreover, many are frustrated at the lack of information that they receive about their child's progress in the early days of attendance at a new school (Hadden and Fowler 1997).

If they are planning for their child to attend a regular school, they may worry about the reaction of other parents, particularly those who may be concerned that their non-disabled children might not receive adequate attention in the face of the increased demands from the child with special needs; and the parents themselves recognize that meeting their child's needs may be too much to ask of a teacher who has 30 other children to cater for (Bentley-Williams and Butterfield 1996).

The choice of school is a great concern for parents. Like all parents, they have to adjust to the notion that no school is going to provide all that their child requires. However, there is likely to be an even greater than usual disparity between their disabled child's needs and the schooling options that are available. Furthermore, while the school's concern may be primarily academic, most parents 'just want their child to be happy' at school. If the child becomes socially isolated at school, it is the parents who have to console their child every evening and force him or her to school every morning. If the child is not keeping up academically, it is the parents who have somehow to bolster their child's self-esteem in the face of constant failure. Both of these problems can be more acute in regular schools than in special schools; and yet parents may feel that attendance at a special facility might not expose the child to the usual social graces that they can learn from non-disabled peers in a regular stream. Such is the choice they face.

Older siblings can find this period difficult, especially if their brother or sister begins to attend their school and so his or her problems are now 'public'. They will need additional information about their siblings' disability and will need to know what words to use to explain it to peers (Alper et al. 1995). Another issue is that whereas once school was a respite from their responsibility to care for and protect their disabled sibling, now this role can extend to school as well. Most can accommodate this with support, but they also need permission to look after their own needs as well.

Parents of non-disabled children find that their involvement with their children peaks in the primary school years as they act as taxi driver to extracurricular and social activities. In comparison, parents of children with disabilities have been doing this for many years prior to school commencement, and might seek to reduce this once their child is in school (Mallory 1996). Instead, however, they can face extra demands of organizing or even supporting their child's participation in extracurricular activities (Alper et al. 1995).

These reactions depend significantly on the range and quality of services that are available to the children: if these fit the children's needs well, then this transition is naturally less painful than if the services do not match what the children require.

Adolescence

As the young person with a disability grows older, the gap between expected development and reality becomes more stark (Hughes and May

1988). The lack of independence of a disabled adolescent can be a painful reminder of the young person's failure to achieve the earlier developmental tasks of childhood (Seligman and Darling 1997). As at the earlier stage of entry to school, if the parents had thought that 'normal' education would make their child 'normal' and this has not occurred, the move to high school can be accompanied by disappointment and confusion (Lovitt and Cushing 1999).

Whereas the children's caretaking demands do decrease compared with early childhood, these are nevertheless considerably higher than is expected at this age for children without disabilities (Haveman et al. 1997). This is especially so when the young people lack adaptive skills, have behavioural difficulties, or have chronic health problems (Haveman et al. 1997).

Suitability of school and peer acceptance determine the level of stress the young person brings home at the end of each school day and, therefore, the extent to which parents and siblings will feel stressed in response.

At the same time as the stage of adolescence brings new challenges, by now the parents are experienced at parenting and at negotiating the service system (Hughes and May 1988). Their successes to date will have given them confidence. Their goals may be less ambitious and by now they are more likely to be 'taking one day at a time' (Hughes and May 1988). These reactions characterize adjustment to the needs of their son or daughter (Haveman et al. 1997).

Alternatively, exhaustion can have set in. Parents may passively accept with resignation the limited services that are available to them and fatalistically do not question why these are so inadequate (Hughes and May 1988). These competing effects have been termed the 'wear and tear' effects.

Parents' expectations of their children's ultimate level of education is not affected by the presence or absence of a disability as such, but by the children's actual school achievements (Masino and Hodapp 1996). Depending on their child's achievement levels, parents whose son or daughter has a disability may not experience the stage of anticipating independence until their offspring is well into adulthood: some families struggle permanently to adjust both to the transition to independence, and also to the lack of adult services and support. In the absence of appropriate support, they may be reluctant to endorse preparatory training for the independence of their son or daughter.

Beginning adult life

A young person's disability means that his or her family is not in the same stage of the family life cycle as other parents with similar-aged sons and daughters. Just as non-disabled adolescents are getting ready to leave home, once again the family whose son or daughter has a disability have to redouble their efforts to secure employment or independent housing for their near-adult child. They have to become more rather than less involved, especially when adult services are 'inadequate, unavailable, or unacceptable' (Thorin et al. 1996: 117). This increased involvement at early adulthood can isolate them from other families.

Parents' attitudes to the transition from school to work and their comfort with their son's or daughter's increased independence may be affected by:

- their comfort with the transition process in general;
- their vision of their son's or daughter's future;
- their assessment of the degree of preparation for adulthood that their child has received from school;
- the perceived level of support in the new placement;
- their ability to provide ongoing emotional and other support in the future (Whitney-Thomas and Hanley-Maxwell 1996).

Transition process

It is clear that young people with disabilities have a more difficult time making the transition to adulthood than do those without disabilities (Whitney-Thomas & Hanley-Maxwell 1996). Although most families these days are apprehensive for the future employment prospects of their adolescents, when the young person has a disability, this can add another layer of concern and cause considerable anxiety as the family becomes clear about the limited residential, vocational and recreational options for their adult son or daughter (Hughes & May 1988).

Vision

Parents of children with disabilities are less optimistic about their children's adult futures than is so when the young people do not have disabilities (Whitney-Thomas and Hanley-Maxwell 1996). In one study, over half of the parents surveyed thought that it was unlikely that their son or daughter with severe disabilities would gain employment (Kraemer et al. 1997). While wanting their adult son or daughter to develop a sense of independence, parents often realize that he or she will need continued support (Whitney-Thomas & Hanley-Maxwell 1996).

Response to school services

At the same time as their child moves services, the parents are experiencing an institutional transition themselves: they are having to leave behind a familiar routine, a service (school), and supportive practitioners on whom they have relied for many years (Hughes and May 1988). Their son' or daughter's teachers have given prolonged practical support – not the least of which is respite care – and so it is to teachers that parents continue to look for support, over and above general medical practitioners or the social welfare workers whom they are about to encounter again (Hughes and May 1988).

Perceived support in adult life

As with beginning school, reactions to the stage of leaving school are determined by the quality of services available, rather than the person's disability as such. However, at this time of most acute need, there are few services available (Hughes and May 1988).

As well as the presence or absence of suitable services, parents also engage in 'risk assessment': they have to balance how much independence to give their son or daughter compared with how much risk is involved (Thorin et al. 1996). When teachers are trying to encourage parents to allow their adult son or daughter more independence, it pays to be aware that the support that is available at school is not necessarily present in the community setting and so, although teachers may regard the young person as capable of achieving at high levels, the parents may disagree as a result of their assessment that there is insufficient support for independence in the community (Voelker et al. 1997).

Ability to support their son or daughter in future

Parents of young adults with disabilities are commonly concerned about their son' or daughter's inactivity and social isolation after school (Lehmann and Roberto 1996), and their consequent reliance on the family to provide social contacts with the community. They want their adult children to have a social life independent of them (Thorin et al. 1996).

Not only do they want their adult son or daughter to become independent for his or her own sake, but parents also seek some independence for themselves after many years of basing their decisions about their own lives on how these would affect their child (Thorin et al. 1996). Yet this is a double bind: some report that they are too tired and risk burnout if they were to teach their children independent skills; and yet, if they do not, they guarantee that their children remain reliant on them (Thorin et al. 1996).

A particularly personal challenge that parents of young adults report is that they want to accept their children as they are and not force them to conform to normative patterns of adult life if that is not what the children want (Thorin et al. 1996). They cannot predict what their children are capable of and so want to encourage them to achieve as much independence as possible, but they do not want failure to crush their son or daughter either (Thorin et al. 1996).

In my work (Louise) with young people who were in the transition to adulthood, professionals sometimes overlooked this complexity of parents' emotions, characterizing them as 'over-protective'. This is much too simple an understanding of the many dilemmas that parents struggle with and the intensity with which they feel them. The first step to addressing their concerns will be to label them sensitively and then to work with the parents to address the issues that are a concern for them, rather than having the parents deal with our agenda (Thorin et al. 1996). Meanwhile, as at any other stage, it will be important not to compound the parents' difficulties with any additional stressors or crises (Thorin et al. 1996).

Maintaining adult life

As this text is directed towards those who are working with children who have special needs, we will not say much here about the stage of adult life. However, in planning for life beyond the school years, it can help to know that the major concern in this life phase is what will happen to the adult son or daughter when the parents die or become too infirm to continue care. Adult siblings may feel pressure to take up the ongoing care, regardless of their wishes. It is at this time that community support services are particularly needed, and yet they are least available and accessible (Seligman and Darling 1997).

Transition periods

Although there are times when the family may be dominated by a child's disability and how best to meet his or her consequent needs, on the whole, this is not the family's only focus throughout life (Hughes and May 1988). The times when the disability is most likely to be a central concern are the times of transition between life stages. This can be particularly so for families with a child who has a disability, for a range of reasons.

- Anticipated changes can re-acquaint the parents with their initial feelings about their child's disability at the time of identification, especially if they have fears about the child's readiness to move to the next developmental stage or service.
- The transitions might not occur at the same ages as for non-disabled children. Their timing is not as easy to predict, and so family members cannot fully prepare in advance for upcoming changes.
- Planning too far in advance can add to parental stress, rather than reduce it.

- The parents and professionals might not know ahead of time what the child's needs will be in a few months or years, and thus what services (if available) would be suitable.
- When they move on, families must abandon one service system that they know in favour of another that is unfamiliar.
- The new service might not meet the child's needs as well as the first service – for instance, in South Australia remedial programmes in schools are less extensive than in preschools and so parents might not be 'grieving' so much about their child's disabilities as about the inability of a new service to cater adequately for those needs.

It is no wonder, therefore, given these uncertainties and impoverished services, that, as Seligman and Darling (1997: 24) report

> As a disabled child approaches critical periods, parents may experience renewed anxiety or sadness.

Nevertheless, most families are able to negotiate these transitions, especially when parents are clear of their goals and can plan for change ahead of time (Turnbull and Turnbull 1997). However, this is complicated by the fact that, during transitions, families also experience what Mallory (1996) termed 'institutional change'. This involves moving from one service system to another. As with non-disabled children, most of these changes will be dictated by age, but some will be independent of age and instead are controlled by the institutions. Such changes will involve, say, moving from a regular school to a special school or moving out of home into group accommodation. Sometimes, this move is not a private matter for the person concerned and his or her family, but can become a subject of bureaucratic decisions, such as when the state assumes guardianship over an adult with disabilities (Mallory 1996). This, then, adds another layer of complexity to the family's planning for transitions. Entry criteria and waiting lists prolong the tension about whether their son or daughter will be admitted to a new service. In this way, it is not the parents' own wishes that take precedence but the decisions of the service providers. Thus, at times of institutional transition, parents are more prone to feeling powerless, anxious and tense (Hughes and May 1988), creating fertile ground for conflict between them and service providers.

Conclusion: Support through the family life cycle

The quality of social support is a key factor in a family's adjustment to any life crisis. Suelzle and Keenan (1981, in Seligman and Darling 1997) found that needs for support services were highest at preschool and young adult ages, although the need for respite care was fairly constant throughout school age, according to DeMyer and Goldberg (1983, in Seligman and Darling 1997). As may be expected, practical issues tend to become paramount as the children grow older, whereas coping difficulties are most evident at the time that the child's disability is first discovered. Even so, the types of practical issues with which families need support will differ more in degree than in type from families without a disabled child, and reflect the usual functions that all families fulfil.

Summary and implications for professionals

All families face natural challenges according to the life stage in which they are functioning. As families move through the life cycle, the demands on their resources wax and wane, making it possible at some times for them to be actively involved in their child's special services, while making this extremely difficult at other times.

As we also saw in Chapter 2, the ability of some families to face additional challenges – such as the identification of their child's disability – might already be compromised by their living circumstances at the time. Families who are coping with external pressures – such as long working hours, prolonged poverty or unemployment – could find that, willing though they are, they have no additional resources (financial, time, or emotional) to commit to a special programme for their child.

The implications for professionals who work with children and their families are that we can help maintain the integrity of families by being aware of the multiple challenges that they may be facing and the many everyday tasks they are already achieving, and by being sure not to add to the demands on them at times when they are not able to take on any more commitments.

Discussion questions

1. Which family function do parents report to you is most affected by their child's special needs? In what ways is the impact positive for the family? In what ways do they experience its impact negatively?
2. How can your service help parents to plan for and negotiate their child's transition to the next service or stage of life?
3. In your experience, what additional support do you think that families need during the various life stages or at transitions between stages?

Chapter 4
The experience of parenting children with disabilities

> . . . our family is a complex system, as are all other families. We have our times of great joy and victory, as well as our moments of frustration and despair. We have periods when we are managing well the stress of living with children who have very special needs, and other periods when we are not coping well at all. And yet, as we meet other families, families who don't have children with labels, we find that all families seem to go through these periods of strengths and difficulties. In seeing this, we are reinforced in our belief that our most potent strategy for enhancing the health and well-being of our family is to think of ourselves and our child as 'normal' and to lead a normal life.
>
> Lusthaus and Lusthaus (1993: 50)

Key points

- To work collaboratively with parents who have children with disabilities you will find it invaluable to have a sound understanding of their experience as parents.
- The influence of disability on families and individuals is complex and therefore we should not assume that all parents will experience their family in the same way.
- Parenting children with disabilities never occurs in a vacuum: each family lives within a social environment. It may be the circumstances of this environment rather than the disability itself which presents difficulties for families. (For example, there may be poor community acceptance of disability or services may not be available.)

Introduction

The role of parent brings many changes to people's lives, while the experience of parenting itself can give rise to the full gamut of emotional responses. In these respects families who have children with disabilities are no different from any others. Yet there are many factors surrounding disability that may alter the experience of parenting and, in turn, people's responses to it.

For instance, parents who have children with disabilities are likely to have considerable contact with professionals and services in relation to their child. This intense involvement with professionals is not the norm for most families. Overlaying this, some of the characteristics and needs of children who have disabilities place heavy demands on parental resources and relationships.

It should also be remembered that the role of parent is usually only one of the roles that individuals fulfil. They are likely to balance this role with many others including that of partner (if they have one), sibling, son or daughter, friend and possibly employer or employee. And they also have personal needs which warrant attention. Therefore, while we as professionals might focus on the parenting role for people who have children with disabilities, we also need to understand them as people who are engaged in a range of relationships, and who operate in the context of multiple responsibilities and needs (including their own).

The aim of this chapter, then, is to identify the potential reactions of parents and also examine how adults adjust to the responsibilities and demands associated with their parenting role. We would be making crude generalizations if we claimed that all parents who have children with disabilities feel a certain way or find a particular situation difficult. Therefore, we must keep in mind that parents of children with disabilities are individuals, and that respecting them begins with recognition that they are comparable to ourselves in complexity and uniqueness (Hayes 1998).

Research into families with a child who has a disability

Prior to describing parents' experience of having a child with a disability, we need to qualify the information about their reactions. Society as a whole has viewed disability negatively and researchers have tended to mirror that perception (Summers et al. 1989). With these preconceived views in place, the questions that researchers ask of parents mainly focus on the negative side of their experiences (Turnbull et al. 1998). For instance, if researchers assume that families with a child with a disability are likely to experience increased stress, they will ask questions about parents' stressors and perhaps use only those instruments that allow for measurement of pathology (Glidden 1993, in Sandler and Mistretta 1998). This is understandable, as much of the research in this field is aimed at advocating for services for those families who need them (Helff and Glidden 1998), but it biases our understanding of these families in general.

The other factor that taints what we know about families whose child has a disability is that researchers have tended to ask middle-class parents, as these parents are most readily accessible. As we discuss in this chapter, these might be the very families who feel most disappointment about their child's forfeited potential, whereas other families might not experience the same sense of personal loss. Furthermore, when there is a large difference in status between researchers and families, as is the case when families are poor or from an otherwise stigmatized group, they are unlikely to tell researchers that the questions being asked are not relevant to them (Harry 1996).

Guided by the research and background attitudes to disability, practice does little to contradict professionals' assumption that disability is predominantly negative, as service providers tend to be approached by families only in times of difficulty or crisis. This contact with parents during times of challenge may reinforce practitioners' assumptions about the negative effects of disability on families, with the result that they explicitly or implicitly convey this view to parents.

Despite the large number of studies involving families and disability, the research can support only the very general statements that families' responses can be due to the interaction of many parent, child, and ecological variables, and that the presence or absence of certain of these factors still cannot lead to sound predictions of family outcomes, as human interaction is so complex (Landesman et al. 1989).

Parental reactions

The birth of a child with a disability can be understood to be a non-normative event, which means that it does not occur in the lives of most people (Baltes 1987). This notion links the unexpectedness of disability with feelings of loss and disappointment, although parents who have their child's disability confirmed after a long period of concern clearly find the diagnosis less unexpected than those whose child is born with readily identifiable disabilities or who acquires an impairment suddenly through trauma.

Grief, loss and chronic sorrow

In the past, the disability literature has said that parents grieve about their child's disability in similar stages as occur after any loss (Solnit and Stark 1961). However, it is now acknowledged that parents may experience feelings from any of the 'stages' at any time: there is not a linear progression. For example, Cameron and colleagues (1992) found that emotions emerged and re-emerged at significant life events (birthdays, starting school, etc) and at frustration with delays in services.

Parents who grieve about their child's disability – and not all do – might react to the child's diagnosis as if they have lost their fantasized 'normal' baby. These parents must say goodbye to this fantasy, while maintaining ongoing care for the child who may seem to be a stranger to them. Their sense of loss may resemble feelings at the death of a family member, although with a major difference that parents may not give themselves sufficient time to grieve, as they must respond to the child's daily care needs rather than to their own emotional requirements.

For those parents who do grieve about their child's disability, their reactions will be unique. Some may find that they experience a whole range of feelings close together in time. Others might find that their grief is never 'resolved' as we understand it but that, instead, it might be re-visited – at times of transition, or when the parents see their child in the company of non-disabled children (McKenzie 1996). Olshansky (1962) termed this 'chronic sorrow'. Yet he notes that the sadness does not preclude parents from feeling satisfaction and joy at their child's achievements and that, 'every parent . . . accepts and rejects the child at various times and in various situations' (Olshansky 1962: 12). This is probably as true for parents of non-disabled children as for parents of children with disabilities.

Parental grief may also be related to the changes in circumstances that the child's disability and community reactions to it bring for the parents. For instance, parents may grieve over their devalued status in the community because they have produced a child who is less valued. They may grieve for the loss of control over their own circumstances because they now have to defer to the decisions of government agencies or service professionals. Or they may grieve about the changes in their own personal circumstances; for example, if they have chosen to care for their child at home, they may feel the loss of career advancement or employment satisfaction. The point is that parents may not grieve so much for the loss of the child they expected, as for the personal restrictions that the child's disability imposes on their own lives.

Anderegg and colleagues (1992) re-conceptualize the grief cycle into three phases which they label confronting, adjusting and adapting. The three stages involve the following components:

- Confronting, which may involve shock and denial, blame and guilt;
- Adjusting, which may involve depression, anger and bargaining; and
- Adapting, which may comprise a change of lifestyle, realistic planning and altered expectations.

Confronting

In this phase, the parents' main difficulty is not necessarily acute shock at the child's diagnosis but the 'chronic sorrow' (Olshansky 1962) of their daily struggle to meet the needs of their child while maintaining their self-esteem as people, their integrity as a family, and their place in the community. For some, this grief reaction will be clearly observable; for others, its absence might be remarked upon and attributed to their denial of their child's difficulties. However, the absence of grief or sorrow and the appearance of optimism is not unusual and professionals must not be too hasty to dismiss an optimistic parent as being 'in denial'. Just because the parents disagree with you about what their child can achieve, this does not mean that they deny the reality of their child's condition. The parents have more evidence of the child's capabilities than you are able to observe; they might just be maintaining the hope that is necessary for them to survive; or you might be wrong about the child's potential.

The 'shopping behaviour' of which some parents are accused may seem to be due to denial. It involves seeing a succession of professionals, seeking one with the expertise to assist the child. However, this may not represent a lack of adjustment but may be a legitimate response to the inappropriateness of present services.

Mothers may feel guilt in response to their child's disability and especially worry that their actions – that something they did or did not do, either during pregnancy or later (say, if the child's disability were the result of an accident) – may have contributed to the disability. It may help to remind them that if they could have done something to prevent it, they would have or, in the case of an inherited disability, that they too inherited their genes and obviously are not to blame for having done so.

Blame is another aspect of the confronting stage. Parents may find fault with others, especially professionals – for instance the obstetrician whose lateness in attending the birth probably was unrelated to the child's condition but is seen by the parent to have been the cause of the child's subsequent problems.

Adjusting

At times, parents may feel utter depression and isolation: they are sure that no one else has ever experienced what they are going through. The loneliness can be exacerbated by the child's high caretaking needs or numerous professional appointments that take time which otherwise the parents could have used to maintain contact with friends. For this reason, professionals must avoid making excessive demands on parents' time.

Anger can occur at the realization that their child will not improve significantly, or that the services cannot be tailor-made to suit their child's needs perfectly. This can bring about criticism of anyone who has been or is involved in the child's care and who has been unable to 'cure' the child's disability. At this time, it is important for professionals not to take the parents' anger personally and to accept that it is a healthy part of the process of having to adjust to the realities of an imperfect service system. This also highlights that parents are not necessarily adjusting to their 'child' but to the circumstances in which they will have to raise him or her.

Another aspect of the adjusting process is bargaining. This may be characterized by slavish adherence to demanding intervention programmes, as if in the hope that, 'If only I work hard enough now, my child will attain a normal level of development.'

Adapting

Confronting, adjusting and adapting can be understood as ongoing processes. Although the terms 'well-adjusted' and 'positive adaptation' tend to suggest that the process of responding to circumstances has been successful, parents often describe themselves as never really adapting but coming to a stage where they feel more in control of their circumstances: that they can manage whatever comes their way by calling on their own resources (including their past experiences of managing) and support from other sources.

It could also be argued that parents never really come to a stage where they have accepted their child's disability. We wonder whether it is too much to ask or expect of parents, not least because they do not necessarily continue to feel sad or sorry for themselves but sad for their child – for the missed opportunities and limitations that disability places on their child and the limitations that societies impose on people with disabilities (Sandler and Mistretta 1998). Parents of any child would give their life to protect their child from harm, and these parents have heartfelt regret that they could not protect their child from his or her disability.

A final word on grief, loss and chronic sorrow

The models which describe parents' reactions to disability are useful in that they can provide frameworks for understanding parents' emotions. As such, they may have clinical application (in counselling, for example). However, parental reaction to disability is unlikely to follow a predetermined sequence of stages. Grief models may encourage stereotyping of parents' reactions to disability and lead professionals to believe that all parents follow a characteristic course, but some parents will have such reactions, while others will not. It is appropriate to have knowledge of these models (because awareness may help us to understand the reactions of some individuals) but it is inappropriate to impose these models onto parents. The following quotation from a mother illustrates this point (McKenzie 1995: 8):

> I remember the paediatrician saying, 'I suppose you must have shed quite a few tears over this,' and I said, 'No I haven't shed a single tear'. I mean it never occurred to me to cry about it and I just, I don't know, perhaps I should've! And the geneticist said, 'You know this is none of your fault, there's nothing you could have done to prevent . . .' And it never occurred to me that it could have been my fault and then I started thinking, 'Oh what did I do wrong during pregnancy that could have caused this.' Up until they suggested it, it never occurred to me that there was anything that I could have done. I just took it as it came.

It appears that the paediatrician in this case was attempting to show understanding of how this mother might be feeling (possibly sorrowful) and the geneticist appeared to be attempting to alleviate any feelings of guilt that she might have had. However, for this mother, it appears that they either misinterpreted or pre-empted her feelings. This example illustrates that some parents who have children with disabilities will feel sorrow or guilt, but individual people will have individual reactions. Professionals need to be mindful of this.

Stress

Parental stress in families who have a disabled member is one of the most frequently researched topics within the disability literature. The aim of the research is to find out how services could intervene to support families. For instance, Glidden and Floyd (1997) indicate that some of what is generically labelled as stress for parents may actually be depression – which changes our understanding of the forms of support needed by these families.

The stress reaction is a physical response in the body involving four stages: an adrenalin-based alarm reaction when a threat is first perceived; appraisal of the situation; search for a coping strategy; and implementation of the selected strategy (Honig 1986). Stressors are specific external or internal demands which we believe tax or exceed our ability to cope (Compas 1987). Most events that are considered to be stressors are negative changes in individuals' lives that are largely beyond their control (Slee 1991). These can be everyday hassles or traumatic life events (Luthar and Zigler 1991). As to the latter, traumatic life events will have different effects depending on when they occur in a person's life; how recently they occurred; whether they are one-off events or chronic life conditions such as poverty; and whether they are internal to the individual (e. g. an illness) or arise from external sources such as unemployment (Rutter 1985).

All families experience stress from a range of sources, which can be exacerbated when a child in the family has a disability:

1. Competing demands – from spouse, children, family of origin, or from society. When a child's disability creates extra caretaking – and particularly when this rests on the shoulders of just one parent – that parent may be left with inadequate amounts of time and energy for meeting his or her own needs and those of other family members.
2. Ambiguous expectations. Anxiety about parenting 'the right way' is a new phenomenon putting additional pressure on many modern parents; this can be exacerbated when the child's exact needs are uncertain and when parents place unrealistic expectations on themselves about meeting all of their child's atypical needs.
3. Conditions of hopelessness. When families endure conditions such as chronic poverty, long-term unemployment, or unremitting caretaking, they can become stressed. Financial pressures to meet children's additional needs can impose long or unusual working hours on one parent or can make it difficult for a parent to return to paid work, thus trapping the family in poverty. Meanwhile, marital discord within the family can impede the parents' ability to resolve any such problems.
4. Loss of contact and isolation can stress any family; the reactions of outsiders to a child's disability can exacerbate a family's isolation. Society expects parents to parent well, and yet when they have little support for doing so, they are more likely to become stressed, with resulting depletion of their parenting skills.
5. Stress in society can affect the functioning of families by making child care unaffordable, imposing financial pressures on families, or offering insufficient informal support for parents with dependent children.

Thus, some stress may be child-related; other stressors arise from the parents themselves such as when they blame themselves for their child's disability; and still others are due to the family's circumstances. Together, any one or a combination of these stressors can reduce parents' confidence in themselves and their ability to meet the needs of all family members. But we cannot assume that the presence of a child with a disability is their only cause.

Neither can we assume that any stress that families may experience will be dysfunctional; over short periods it may help them to adapt or it might trigger a search for more appropriate services (Turnbull and Turnbull 1997). Therefore, if a family is experiencing stress, the issues become how intensive and how prolonged is the family's stress and whether the family members are taking productive steps to manage the stress.

Resilience

Another concept that we need to define in order to discuss stress is the notion of resilience. Although many studies have shown that families of children with disabilities experience more stress than other families, these heightened stress levels do not necessarily affect the family's functioning (Dyson 1991, 1993). The fact that so many people cope with adverse circumstances is often attributed to their 'resilience'.

Resilience refers to the ability of families or individuals to withstand stressors and to adjust and adapt to stressful circumstances (see McCubbin and McCubbin 1988; Singer and Powers 1993; Zimmerman and Arunkumar 1994). It is the ability to bounce back from adverse experiences (Bland et al. 1994). Strong families are those who can solve their own problems and, when they become aware that they lack the internal resources for doing so, are able to gain support from outside (Dunst et al. 1988).

Patterson (1991) refers to nine aspects of family resilience in response to disability which include: balancing the demands provoked by the disability with other family needs; maintaining clear family boundaries; developing communication skills; attributing positive meanings to the situation; maintaining family flexibility; maintaining commitment to the family as a unit; engaging in active coping efforts; maintaining social integration; and developing collaborative relationships with professionals.

Seligman and Darling (1997) conclude that it is crucial that professionals are aware of these variables that may affect family adjustment, and that they take the stressors into account when they plan to place any additional demands on family members.

Coping

Coping is the process of changing our thinking or behaviour to manage stressors – that is, to minimize our distress and maximize our performance (Compas 1987). This occurs in a number of stages, as we first appraise the stressor and our own resources for coping with it and then take action (Ryan 1989).

People's appraisal of their situations has much to do with whether they are said to cope or adjust well to challenging circumstances. For example, those parents who seem to cope best with children with disabilities believe that they have control over their circumstances (McKenzie 1996; Scorgie et al. 1998), and this perception, in turn, affects how they respond.

When parents think positively or use the way they think to manage situations it is termed 'cognitive coping' (Turnbull and Turnbull 1993). Cognitive coping was used successfully by over 90% of the parents surveyed in one study (Sandler and Mistretta 1998: 128), who reported using such strategies as 'taking one day at a time, comparing one's situation favourably to that of others and selectively attending to the positive factors in a situation' as helpful. On the other hand, passive appraisal of a situation, such as hoping a problem will go away or hiding one's feelings from others is believed to impact negatively on a family's ability to cope (Judge 1998).

The coping strategy that we use can be problem-focused – that is, we will try to change our circumstances; or it can be emotion-focused – that is, directed at our own emotional reactions. Individuals' methods of coping might vary with time and context depending on the nature of the stressor (Compas 1987); one study also found a difference between parents in that mothers were more likely to use emotion-focused coping strategies and fathers were more likely to use problem-focused strategies (Kravetz et al. 1993). However, the most effective coping style is likely to be one that is flexible and adaptive to circumstances (Compas 1987).

Mothers

Mothers are more active in their child's care and bear most of the burden associated with it (Hassiotis 1997; Heller et al. 1997). Mothers tend to give themselves little time to adjust, as the child with the disability continues to require ongoing care. They typically feel more responsible for the child, are unclear what to expect of the child and themselves, and may doubt their ability to care for a child with special needs. It has also been suggested that the move away from institutionalized care for people with disabilities has increased the burden of care for mothers (Bright and Wright 1986). Mothers are also likely to become concerned about the emotional strain in the family brought about by the child's caretaking demands and other needs, particularly when these are anticipated to persist for their entire life (Koegel et al. 1992).

Bright and Wright (1986: 226) note the contradictions mothers can feel when caring for their children with disabilities:

> At the heart of any attempt to understand the role of mothers of children with disabilities is a need to appreciate that the deep and profound love and concern for their children, and commitment to their future, often places them in conflict with the active pursuit of satisfying their own individual needs and expectations.

Research has indicated that the perceptions of single mothers of rearing a child with a developmental disability are not necessarily very different from those of their married counterparts apart from the possibility that sole parenting may reduce the amount of income coming into the home (Schilling et al. 1986). It is significant that the presence of fathers in the families might not necessarily result in a decrease in the perceived caretaking burden for mothers (Erickson and Upshur 1989).

Mothers often bear the responsibility for carrying out therapies with or teaching their children (Padeliadu 1998). One study revealed that the more time mothers spent in such activities with their child, the more intense were their ratings of family problems (Harris and McHale 1989). This is significant when viewed in regard to the demands that early inter-vention programmes may place on families.

Mothers also tend to be the partner who deals with professionals and attends service appointments. These demands expand their parenting role and can absorb significant amounts of their time and energy. This also means that they need to interpret information from professionals and pass it on to their partners.

As mothers are usually the ones who deal with professionals, this makes them more vulnerable than fathers to the potential negative outcomes of professional contact and system abuse (as discussed in Chapter 3). I (Susan) found an example of this when I was conducting some research: One mother was keen to find a cause for her son's delayed development and unusual behaviour. After a few professional appointments she was frustrated at 'getting nowhere'. Then, at an appointment with the paediatri-cian, he announced: 'I think he's got an anxiety disorder – you're anxious yourself'. This mother did not take kindly to being labelled as anxious and explained: 'The speech therapist was anxious – we all were – but I was only anxious because they couldn't say or didn't know what the problem was'. This example reminds us that it may not be the child who causes stress for parents but the need to deal with a range of professionals.

A mother's self-esteem is often seriously affected by a disabled infant's delay in communicating to her that she is loved. The child's delayed communication skills can make interaction and bonding difficult. This inability to reward the mother for her caretaking efforts may lead to fewer and less positive interactions, consequent reduction in infant stimulation, and further delay in the child's development. However, it is clear that this is a result of the child's disability, not its cause.

While there are similarities between the reactions of mothers to disability, there is also variation. Therefore we must keep in mind that any individual mother's reactions will be personal to her and cannot be predicted with certainty.

Fathers

Much has been written about fathers and their reactions to disability in their children, although the research evidence is scant and much of it is very dated. Some of the research indicates that fathers' concerns at diagnosis typically centre on the long-term issues such as financial concerns, in contrast to mothers who tend to focus on day-to-day care issues.

Like mothers, fathers can experience low self-esteem at the recognition of their child's disability, although fathers' loss of self-esteem is still less marked than for mothers. More recent studies show that fathers may adjust more favourably now than in the past (Seligman and Darling 1997).

Fathers can often withdraw emotionally or seek outlets outside of the home to compensate for their reactions. Their ability to withdraw may allow them to minimize the significance of the child's developmental delays for longer than mothers. In the meantime, if the mother is struggling to achieve a diagnosis, she may feel unsupported both professionally and at home.

Men often report resentment of diagnosing doctors, finding them unsympathetic and abrupt, and they dislike being unable to fix their child, having to rely instead on professionals.

Fathers are not affected by their child's age (Hornby 1994) but are reported to be more affected by the visibility of the disability, and by the social embarrassment that a visible disability can induce. Some report a lack of gratification in their relationship with their disabled son or daughter.

Unless they receive professional support, fathers' negative reactions may continue, to the detriment of their own emotional wellbeing and, indirectly, that of their entire family. Fathers need to be included in services because they can be in pain also, and because otherwise they might get the implicit message that they do not matter and are not expected to react to their child's disability and have nothing to contribute to remedial services. Most importantly, professionals who work with families should avoid projecting onto fathers the low expectations of them and negative characterizations of their reactions that are found in the literature, as these are based on inadequate research evidence (Hornby 1994).

The couple relationship

Some studies support the claim that disability has negative effects on couple relationships while others report that these are strengthened by the presence of a child with a disability (Benson and Gross 1989; Seligman and Darling 1997). Many parents report that their relationship with their partner grows stronger and more intimate as a result of sharing and overcoming the challenges of parenting a child with special needs (Abbott and Meredith 1986) and some describe their partner as a strong source of strength and support (McKenzie 1996).

On the other hand, awareness that their child has a disability can excite powerful emotions in both parents (Featherstone 1980, in Turnbull and Turnbull 1997) and the couple might see the disability as a symbol of their shared 'failure'. Further, the lack of clarity about their child's future, along with other difficulties that may arise in parenting their child, provides a fertile ground for conflict between partners. Meanwhile, the child's high caretaking needs may cause parents to postpone resolving their differences.

The reason that some marriages do not withstand the extra demands of caring for a child with a disability, could be that the conflict around the child's disability merely exacerbates marital problems that were already present, and which block partners' ability to resolve the issues of the child's care. Further, it may be that professional involvement can divert parents' attention away from marital issues towards meeting the needs of the disabled child, with the result that the needs of the relationship are neglected to the point where it is no longer sustainable (Harris 1983, in Seligman and Darling 1997).

Thus, parental separation could be caused by a number of factors unrelated to the presence of the child but, like any additional demands, the child's special needs represent the 'straw that breaks the camel's back' (McKenzie 1996). The separation of parents with non-disabled children is not blamed on the children; the same should be so when a child in the family has special needs.

When professionals neglect to support fathers, they are ignoring the importance of fathers to the couple relationship and thus may be placing the relationship under extra pressure. Further, professionals can develop an unusual bond with mothers, rendering fathers something of a 'spare wheel' in the family, as no family requires three parents. It is no wonder, then, that some fathers, finding themselves redundant in their own family, choose to withdraw emotionally or even leave altogether.

In summary, 'issues associated with the exceptionality can simultaneously strengthen and impair a couple's relationship' (Turnbull and Turnbull 1997: 99). Further, the mixed research findings suggest that professionals should not assume that the presence of a child with a disability will have an adverse effect on couple relationships.

Contextual factors affecting parental response

How parents respond to the demands of parenting children with disabilities depends on contextual factors both within and outside the family. For instance, such factors as the presence of appropriate services, a supportive partner, a high level of parental education, and financial assistance can alleviate many of the additional demands (Yau and Li-Tsang 1999).

Child characteristics

The experience of parenting children with disabilities will be affected by the children's characteristics and their rate of development along with their anticipated ultimate developmental status (Brinker et al. 1994; Frey et al. 1989; Robbins et al. 1991).

The type of the child's disability will influence parental reactions. For instance, parents of children with Down syndrome may be less stressed than parents whose children have other forms of intellectual (learning) disability (Crank 1990, in Stores et al. 1998).

The child's caretaking demands and ability to perform self-care tasks have an acute effect on parents. Depending on the nature of the child's disability, his or her caretaking needs may not only be chronic but be anticipated to last for years to come (Seligman and Darling 1997). The child's age is also likely to affect parental perceptions of caretaking burden (Erickson and Upshur 1989; Harris and McHale 1989; Heller et al. 1997). As children age some parents grow more pessimistic about their children's future (Scorgie et al. 1998). The children's gender also makes a difference as male children tend to have more behavioural difficulties than females, while parents may have higher expectations of sons, and so on both counts adjust more readily to their daughters' limitations than they do to their sons' (Scorgie et al. 1998).

The child's behaviour can cause considerable strain (Hodapp et al. 1998; Scorgie et al. 1998; Stores et al. 1998; Suarez and Baker 1997; Turnbull and Ruef 1996), especially when it is unpredictable, as this provokes constant vigilance or 'being on call 24 hours a day' (McKenzie 1994; Turnbull and Ruef 1996; Webster-Stratton and Spitzer 1996), which will be exhausting.

The parents will also be affected by their child's ability to communicate, social responsiveness, competence and temperament (Scorgie et al 1998), including emotional disturbances such as the depression that can follow a traumatic head injury.

Meanwhile, the child's prognosis, number of hospital admissions or professional appointments, medication regimes and growth and development, will all influence parental well-being (McKenzie 1996).

Timing of diagnosis

A more severe disability may be apparent at birth; a less severe one may be diagnosed later, sometimes to the relief of parents who have been concerned for some time about the child's apparently abnormal development. Until a diagnosis is delivered, the parents may be struggling to cope with the unknown, and receiving little support. At the same time, though, once the diagnosis is achieved, some parents may feel guilty about having blamed their child in the past for behaviour over which he or she had little control.

Time demands

The nature of the child's disability can influence the time demands placed on parents. Time demands are not only associated with caregiving, but with the child's education, liaison with professionals, attendance at medical appointments and therapy sessions and the numerous tasks that parenting children with disabilities often brings. In order to sustain energy levels parents need a break from 'chronic responsibility' (Turnbull and Ruef 1996).

The demands on parents' time can be understood as an ongoing burden which can wear parents down and lead them to feel they have diminished control over their own circumstances. Mothers of children with Down syndrome may face increased demands on their time on a daily basis (related to recreation and education of children) compared with mothers who have children without disabilities (Padeliadu 1998). Similarly, mothers of children with motor impairments reported that more time was required for caretaking compared with mothers of children without such impairments (Erickson and Upshur 1989).

While some parents find that 'working with' children is demanding in terms of time and energy, they also see it very much as part of their role in caring for children and promoting their children's development. Success at this can contribute to their own wellbeing and positive outlook (McKenzie 1996; Padeliadu 1998). This is an example where more intense responsibilities can lead to difficulties, yet simultaneously have positive outcomes for parents.

Family and social support

The availability of support from family and friends is likely to have an influence on the experience of parenting children with disabilities (Beckman 1991). Such support has the potential to mediate many of the stresses and demands that can be associated with the parenting role. For example, grandparents can provide support to their own son or daughter in caring for children with disabilities (as discussed in Chapter 5).

Trute and Hauch (1988) interviewed parents from families of children with developmental disabilities who were identified as having positively adjusted to the birth of their child. These researchers found that satisfaction with their family support network was high in these families, even though network size was small. The couples had both family members and friends who were available for emotional support, for advice and information, and for social participation.

Involvement with services and professionals

The availability and utilization of professionals' services can influence the experience of parenting children with disabilities. Where services and professionals are perceived as helpful by parents they can be very beneficial for the child and the whole family (McKenzie 1994). However, we know that professional involvement can have both positive and negative outcomes for parents and may turn parents into 'advocates' and 'negotiators' when what they want most of all is to be 'parents' (as discussed in Chapter 1).

Financial demands

Parents of children with disabilities often face increased financial burdens related to their child's needs (Bailey et al. 1992; McKenzie 1994; Rasmussen 1993) which relate to the cost of therapy or special equipment or possibly loss of income as parents make the choice to care for their children full-time rather than work outside of home. This choice may be made because child care staff indicate they can not 'cope' with the child (McKenzie 1993) or because there are no post-school options available. Lack of finance reverberates throughout the family as it limits family activities and opportunities and is an ongoing source of stress for parents (Minnes 1988).

The family's socioeconomic status (SES) can affect parents' ability to meet their needs (as was addressed in Chapter 2). For instance, families with high SES are likely to have more resources to pay for services that are not available through the public sector.

Cultural membership

Various societies and cultures have differing reactions to disability (Seligman and Darling 1997). Cultural membership significantly affects parenting of any children, including those with disabilities. Some cultural beliefs will lead parents to think that their child's disability is a form of punishment, causing them to want to hide the child away from others because of the shame associated with disability. These beliefs will also affect parents' willingness to use available services (as will the cultural sensitivity of the services).

Cultural values will also determine parents' interactions with their children. For example, Greek mothers of children with Down syndrome were found to experience stress associated with their child's educational needs because they spent a large amount of time teaching their children as this was very important to them as Greek parents (Padeliadu 1998). In addition, differences in mother-child interactions have a cultural basis, so a child's interaction pattern may appear alarming in one culture but normative – and therefore acceptable – in another.

Community acceptance of disability

Over and above the social stressors to which any family may be vulnerable, a family with a child with a disability can be subjected to a further major cultural stressor – namely, social stigma (Seligman and Darling 1997). The stigma differs for different disabilities. In conditions that are not immediately obvious, the strain of 'impression management' may be great for parents. In conditions where the disability is visible, some parents find that other people put up a pretence of accepting the child or family, while their interactions remain at a superficial level only. Many researchers report changes in parents' social interactions as a result of social non-acceptance of their child (Cavanagh and Ashman 1985; McKenzie 1994, 1996; Turnbull and Ruef 1996).

In one study, parents identified the move in disability services from segregated to inclusive services and increased community acceptance of disability as having positive outcomes for their own wellbeing (McKenzie 1996). They also found these changes had meant a great deal to them and led to an increasingly positive outlook for both their children's and their own futures. For example, mothers of children with developmental disabilities who attended the local preschool were less pessimistic and more positive about their child's characteristics and their own self-esteem than mothers whose children participated in segregated preschool programmes (Rimmerman and Duvdevany 1995).

Geographic location

Families in rural areas often find they are a long way from services and are disadvantaged by this in terms of the amount of support they are able to secure for themselves and their children. This can be very worrying for parents and some will make the decision to relocate to a city location. This may be beneficial for the child but often involves upheaval for the family and possibly reduced income. The access to services is sometimes gained at the expense of losing friends and family and community support (McKenzie 1996).

Positive outcomes

While research has usually focussed on the anticipated difficulties of parenting a child with a disability, some researchers have attended to the positive contributions that people with disabilities make to their families (see Mullins 1987; Turnbull et al. 1988; Glidden et al. 1988). A focus on the positive contributions that people with disabilities make to their families provides balance to the predominantly negative focus of research concerning these families.

Summers and colleagues (1989: 29) suggest that 'the vast majority of evidence for positive contributions lies not in the empirical literature but in parent narratives and anecdotal literature.' They cite one study (Turnbull and Turnbull 1986) in which parents who had children with and without disabilities were interviewed about areas of their lives that had been affected by their child. The findings indicated that parents of children with disabilities perceived their children as having made similarly positive contributions to their lives as did children without disabilities.

Some parents report that parenting a child with a disability helped them to learn better ways to deal with problems (McLinden 1990, in Sandler and Mistretta 1998). Others acknowledge the positive outcomes of caring for children with disabilities and in one study (Grant et al. 1998) very few carers of family members with disabilities had difficulty identifying rewards from their caregiving experience.

The positive contributions that people with disabilities make to their families as expressed by fathers, siblings and grandparents include: pride in things the child can do, personal strength, family closeness, feelings of happiness and fulfilment, personal growth and maturity and sense of control or influence over events (Meyer 1993; Sandler and Mistretta 1998).

A study of the positive impacts of children with an intellectual disability on families revealed that parents perceived their children as a source of joy and happiness (Stainton and Besser 1998). They also perceived an increase in personal and social networks and community involvement which they attributed to the presence of their children and also described the positive impacts of their children on others and the community.

Nevertheless recognition of positive outcomes does not minimize the challenges that these families can experience but describes the 'perspectives of families who have struggled, persevered, and even thrived – despite the presence of a disability in the family' Meyer (1993: 85).

Attention to the positive contributions of people with disabilities also challenges some commonly held assumptions about these families and could influence the way in which professionals approach them.

Summary

Despite the difficulties that parents of children with disabilities can face and the possible negative effects of disability on parents, these families appear to be more like other families than they are different (Behr and Murphy 1993). Further, parents' reactions that formerly were thought to be a response to the child's disability itself may – at least in part – be a reaction to the mismatch between what services their child needs and what is available. Thus, for instance, anger that may appear to arise because of a child's special needs may instead be an expression of frustration at not being able to get those needs met.

It must also be noted that the parents' difficulties and stress levels might not affect their ability to feel positively about their child. For instance, although parents of children with disabilities report higher stress levels than their counterparts with non-disabled children, nevertheless the two groups of parents report similar levels of positive attitudes to their children (Beckman 1991).

Our awareness of parents' potential reactions to the experience of parenting a child with a disability can help us surmise what challenges they may be facing, but we will inevitably get it wrong if we fail to see each family and each individual as just that – individual. We must listen to what each family tells us of their experiences and offer support and services accordingly, not according to our preconceptions of what they will require.

Discussion questions

1. Consider the way that parents of children with disabilities are portrayed in the media. How do the media perpetuate the stereotypes associated with disability?
2. What could you do in your professional role to accommodate the needs of fathers?
3. Based on the information presented in this chapter about parents' experience of having a child with disabilities, are there any aspects of your own service that you could make more responsive to their needs?

Chapter 5
Beyond parents:
considering the needs of
siblings and grandparents

> In the professional literature and in practice, the term family has increasingly replaced parents (and before that, mothers). This broader focus acknowledges the reciprocal effects a family member's disability or illness can have on all family members. However, despite changes in the terminology, too frequently the word family still refers to 'parents and child with a disability or illness'. Grandparents, aunts and uncles, and siblings are still largely excluded.
>
> Meyer (1993: 88)

Key points

- Sibling relationships usually represent enduring bonds and therefore have the potential to have significant influence on the lives of siblings with and without disabilities.
- Similarly, the grandparenting role and the relationships between grandparents and family members have the potential for positive outcomes for family members.
- There is much we know about the experience of having a sibling or grandchild with a disability, yet there is still much to learn. Nevertheless, we do have information which indicates the ways services and professionals can support both siblings and grandparents in their relationships with family members who have disabilities.

Introduction

So far throughout this book, we have argued that people with disabilities cannot be seen in isolation but need to be understood within the context of their families. Siblings and grandparents often have significant influences on family relationships. Therefore, the inclusion of a chapter on siblings and grandparents is our recognition of the importance of these family members in the lives of individuals with disabilities.

Although your professional role might not involve offering direct support to the brother or sister of a child with a disability, it can be useful to be aware of the different home experiences that such children can bring, say, into the classroom. For instance, some siblings take on home responsibilities beyond their years, in which case you can help by not encouraging them to exercise additional responsibilities at school as well. We need to recognize that siblings have their own special needs, and that meeting these needs is in their interests, as well as those of their brother or sister with a disability.

Siblings

The sibling bond is unique among family relationships in that siblings usually share a common genetic, cultural, and experiential heritage (Pruchno et al. 1996). Despite changes in individual circumstances, sibling relationships have the potential to be the most enduring of all relationships. Whereas parents sometimes leave a family, and families can leave friends, sibling relationships usually endure throughout life, and to a greater age than has been the case in the past. Given that divorce is increasing and geographical moves are common, siblings can be the only source of an ongoing, stable relationship in families. In addition, families now have fewer children and the children are closer together in age, making the sibling relationship more intense. Therefore, there is the potential for a sibling relationship where one of the siblings has a disability to have long-standing influence on the lives of both siblings.

The sense of belonging accompanied by sibling relationships is believed to be important regardless of culture or context (Harry et al. 1998). In any family, sibling relationships are complex, with mixed emotions and, sometimes, less than positive long-term relationship outcomes. This mixed picture is also true when the family has a child with a disability.

Responses of siblings

Having a brother or a sister with a disability may have a positive, neutral or negative effect on siblings, depending on a range factors (Harry et al. 1998; Hannah and Midlarsky 1999). Effects may be felt at some ages and stages in the non-disabled sibling's life but not at others. In addition, there are many conflicting findings. For example, some studies report that siblings experience high levels of stress; others suggest no differences in self-esteem, positive feelings about their lives, or stress when compared with children whose brothers and sisters do not have disabilities (Hannah and Midlarsky 1999). Thus, the picture of sibling responses is complex, influenced, among other things, by the severity and type of the child's disability, the children's ages, birth order, family size and parental influences.

Characteristics of the disability

The characteristics of the sibling who has a disability are believed to have various outcomes for the sibling relationship. The first aspect is the type of disability. For instance, a complex disability, such as autism, may be more confusing for a sibling than a more straightforward diagnosis. Some disabilities will be visible and may attract more stigma, although on the other hand, the unusual behaviour of a child with no outward signs of a disability can cause more embarrassment for siblings than when the child's disability is visible and so excuses the aberrant behaviour. This was borne out in research where adults with siblings who had intellectual (learning) disabilities reported more contact with siblings and more favourable outcomes of the relationships than adults who had siblings with mental illnesses (Seltzer et al. 1997).

The competence level and communication ability of the sibling with the disability is likely to have a profound effect on interactions (Heller et al. 1999). In the case of deaf-blindness the children may have difficulties communicating with each other and may need to use alternative or augmentative communication systems (Heller et al. 1999).

The second aspect to affect siblings' reactions is the severity of their brother's or sister's disability. A child with more severe disabilities may require more caretaking, which can stress the parents – and, in turn, the siblings – and place pressure on siblings to act as substitute carers. On the other hand, the significant factor may not be how much time the child with a disability requires, but how he or she *behaves* when being cared for (Seligman and Darling 1997).

Ages of the children

The sibling relationship where one child has a disability often centres around caretaking, rather than shared play. The level of responsibility that siblings perceive can be related to the birth order and gender of siblings, with elder sisters often shouldering most responsibility. Acting as substitute caretaker takes skill and patience and may limit siblings' opportunities to engage in age-appropriate activities and peer relationships (Hannah and Midlarsky 1999).

Wider spacing between children is reported to lead to less parental stress, and with it less sibling stress. While children of the same gender who are close together in age can feel more companionship, their greater closeness may provide an opportunity for more conflict and embarrassment (Powell and Gallagher 1993).

Siblings who are younger than the child with the disability are particularly prone to misunderstanding the disability and its cause (Lobato 1990), especially if the disability has no visible signs. Younger siblings are also more likely to believe that they will catch the disability, or that they have caused it. They are also in more need themselves of a high degree of nurturing and so they can suffer more than older siblings if that is not available from their parents. Youngest children, however, have grown up with their disabled brother or sister and so may see him or her as normal because that is how it has always been. On the other hand, younger children expect their older brothers and sisters to be more able than them, and may become embarrassed when displays of immature behaviour demonstrate that this is not so. Moreover, once the younger child's development surpasses the older disabled child's, the younger sibling may feel guilty about being more capable than an older sister or brother.

The family's circumstances

The sibling bond is likely to be influenced by particular circumstances of a family system. For example, siblings' perceptions of their parents' attitudes regarding the child with a disability can be a powerful influence on their adjustment (Caldwell and Guze 1960). It seems important for both parents to share the same positive attitude, too, rather than just one parent feeling positive. In addition, the parental and family expectations for siblings to take care of or have responsibility for children with disabilities will also affect the siblings' wellbeing. Although it may be the case that older girls often shoulder this responsibility, it must be remembered that the characteristics of other family members and the cultural background of the family is likely to affect this. It may be that siblings respect and welcome their (sometimes lifelong) responsibility for their brothers or sisters with disabilities as this is a traditional cultural practice. This is particularly the case where families have hierarchical structures and the child with the disability is one of the younger siblings (Harry et al. 1998).

In response to their differing needs, many families treat their disabled and non-disabled children differently. Nevertheless, the non-disabled children may not be dissatisfied with that, perhaps because they believe that it is necessary or fair. That is, more favourable treatment from a parent might not impair a sibling's adjustment. However, siblings do compare how they are treated by parents and evidence that one child is favoured or is given preferential treatment can lead to ill-will and conflict between them (Powell and Gallagher 1993).

Powell and Gallagher (1993) report that children from larger families can be better adjusted than children from smaller families. This may come about because a larger number of children can share extra caretaking tasks and share the pressures to achieve in compensation for the sibling's disability. Further, if there is another non-disabled sibling with whom to share confidences, each sibling is better adjusted than when a sibling has only his or her parents on whom to rely (Lobato 1990).

Size of family influences the family's socioeconomic status (SES), however, which in turn influences the experience of siblings. Families of low SES and larger families may have fewer resources to meet all the caretaking and medical needs of the child, possibly placing more pressure on the family as a whole and increasing the caretaking responsibility of siblings (Hannah and Midlarsky 1999).

Parents from high socioeconomic levels may have difficulty lowering their expectations for a child with a disability, a reaction which siblings might copy. On the other hand, middle-class families often have the funds to pay for outside help, such as a cleaner or housekeeper. This means that parents are freed up to spend more time with the children and can place fewer caretaking demands on their children (Stoneman et al. 1988, in Powell and Gallagher 1993). A higher family income also allows siblings to spend more time in activities away from home, providing friendships and an outlet for their feelings as well as some respite from the demands of home.

Siblings' emotional responses

Children are likely to experience a range of emotions in response to their brother's or sister's disability. However, we must keep in mind that these feelings are not confined to siblings of children with a disability: siblings in any families might frequently have these feelings too (Powell and Gallagher 1993). However, their intensity may be greater with a sibling who has a disability and the feelings themselves might be more persistent, and so the disabled child's brother or sister may need some support to express them.

Young children may be fearful of 'catching' the disability; older children may experience concern about the disabled child's future, at possible exploitation of their brother or sister, about the reaction of their own friends, and fear of having their own children. Many siblings feel different from their peers, that their family is different from others and it is suggested that this feeling of difference may have negative effects on self-esteem and wellbeing (Hannah and Midlarsky 1999).

Siblings may feel isolated from other family members. When another family member is so obviously in need, siblings may be reluctant to ask for their needs to be met. Anger may result from feeling unappreciated and ignored and may be directed towards the disabled brother or sister, parents, society or even God. Children may also feel angry if their mother bears a burden of care without the father's help. They may also feel angry at the parents for not protecting the child from becoming disabled, whether or not they could have prevented it in fact. It is also common for siblings to get angry at peers who mistreat the child with the disability. The extent to which siblings harbour anger depends on a number of factors: how responsible the sibling is for the child with a disability; whether the disabled child manipulates or takes advantage of the sibling; how restricted the sibling's social life becomes; how much parental attention that the child with the disability requires; whether the family can cope financially; and family size (Seligman and Darling 1997).

Siblings may also be angry when their brother or sister is teased and bullied, but may be too frightened themselves in these situations to offer the protection they would wish. Guilt can result from being unable to put a stop to the teasing, even though achieving this is beyond the capabilities of the child's years. If the child's friends are doing the teasing, then loyalty to them can also engender confusion.

Siblings may resent the amount of parental time the child with the disability calls on, resent curtailment of family activities that the disability may provoke, and feel resentful if parental expectations are different for them compared to their disabled brother or sister. Jealousy and resentment can also arise when their disabled brother's or sister's achievements are met with great enthusiasm, whereas their own attainments, appearing to be easier to achieve, are met with a lukewarm response from their parents. Similarly, non-disabled children may resent the amount of school work that they have to do compared with what seems to be more enjoyable learning tasks for the child who has a disability. Jealousy can also lead to guilt for feeling negatively about their sibling, for wanting to have their own needs met and for placing demands on their parents (for 'bothering' them).

Siblings may be embarrassed at the unsightly equipment that their brother or sister uses or might feel embarrassment when his or her inappropriate behaviour attracts attention in public. They sometimes are embarrassed when friends meet their brother or sister for the first time. This can be especially acute, as already mentioned, when the child with the disability is older but does not act it. Sometimes, siblings may not be embarrassed at the reactions of others, but are watchful nevertheless:

> Friends came to our house to play, and I watched to see how they would play with him. As we got older, I tested out the boys I dated to see how they treated Bob. Lots of them just didn't make the cut, because they treated him differently.
>
> Cramer et al. (1997: 46)

Siblings may also be confused about their roles in the family, about the complex feelings that they experience towards their sibling, about treatment priorities for the disabled child, and about parents' different opinions about ways to treat the child. Confusion may be especially felt when the sibling's condition has no known cause and yet results in displays of inappropriate behaviour (such as with autism).

Finally, siblings can feel pressure to achieve at high levels to compensate their parents for the sibling's disability, and eldest girls in particular tend to feel pressure to care for and attend to the disabled sibling both now and in the future.

The negative feelings which we have just described and which are summarized in Table 5.1 are similar to those experienced by parents. These feelings are natural and healthy. It is important that siblings are not forced to deny or try to change them as, like any emotions, they will be transient and are more likely to be resolved if they are accepted as a natural part of life.

Positive aspects of sibling relationships

Having listed siblings' negative feelings, it is important to acknowledge that many also report potent benefits of having a disabled child in the family (Meyer 1993; O'Halloran 1993; Schulz 1993). The differences in children who have disabilities are often celebrated by families (Schulz 1993). These feelings often flow from the parents' and other family members' positive attitudes. The most commonly reported positive outcome is that a child's disability can bring the family closer together.

In terms of their own personal growth, some siblings report that having a child with special needs in the family taught them to accept individual differences (Meyer 1993; Schulz 1993). Positive feelings include strong love and protection, excitement, and joy at their siblings' hard-won achievements. Siblings report that they develop 'greater understanding of people in general and handicaps in particular, more compassion, more sensitivity to prejudice, and more appreciation of their own good health and intelligence' (Grossman 1972, in Lobato 1983: 349; see also Meyer 1993).

Siblings can informally teach their disabled brother or sister skills which the child would not copy from his or her parents. While often feeling pressured to act as a substitute parent or teacher, siblings can also feel some pride and increase in status for taking on these duties. They can gain immense satisfaction from their successes as a 'teacher' and from the hard-won achievements of their brother or sister. Watching a child struggle to learn something which they themselves find easy can teach non-disabled siblings great respect for their disabled sister or brother, and can teach them how to overcome difficulties in their own lives.

Table 5.1: Possible issues encountered by children whose sibling has a disability

	Younger children	Older children
Information	About the disability	About the sibling's education needs About the future
Fears	Of catching the disability Of having caused the disability	About having children themselves
Isolation	From distracted parents	Because of reluctance to ask to have their needs met
Anger	At parental inattention	At mother's work load At parents, for not protecting the sibling from the disability At peers who mistreat their sibling At restrictions on their social life At extra responsibilities
Guilt	About being more capable than their older sibling About their negative feelings	At not being able to protect their sibling from teasing
Resentment	Of differing parental expectations Of receiving lukewarm praise for their own accomplishments, compared with sibling	Of curtailment of family activities
Embarrassment	At special equipment That older sibling does not act more maturely	About anticipated reactions of friends At sibling's inappropriate behaviour About attracting attention in public
Confusion	About the disability especially complex conditions and behaviours About the cause of the disability	About complexity of their own feelings About sibling's treatment priorities About parents' differing opinions on how to treat the child
Pressure	To care for their sibling To include the sibling in their activities	To achieve highly as compensation To take care of sibling To repress their emotions

Children who are actively involved in caring for the child with a disability tend to be well adjusted despite the added responsibilities (Seligman and Darling 1997). Perhaps positive adjustment in siblings is more likely in those families who work as a united team, whereas poor adjustment may be more likely in families where individual siblings feel that they are carrying responsibility *instead of* the parents rather than as an adjunct to them.

Many siblings turn their special sensitivities developed during childhood into a caring career. This is fine, as long as it is not motivated by guilt (Seligman and Darling 1997). Berry (1988) cautions against developing a 'helpaholic' lifestyle where one is addicted to helping others at excessive cost to oneself.

In terms of the relationship between the siblings, Powell and Gallagher (1993) report that even when siblings feel stress or are frustrated with their disabled brothers or sisters, siblings tend not to take out these feelings on them but, if anything, are kind and positive towards them. This restraint may help family functioning and may ensure that the disabled child feels accepted, but it will also need an outlet so that frustration does not become unbearable for siblings.

The siblings can receive an outlet in their relationships with friends when it is accepted that the child with the disability may be left out of some play. When the child with the disability is mainly included in siblings' activities, all family members seem to accept those other occasions when siblings need some time to themselves (Harry et al. 1998). A child's occasional lack of involvement is not seen as a rejection but simply an acknowledgement that he or she is not able to participate.

Interviews with siblings (aged 9–13 years) of younger children with severe disabilities revealed the children's responses were predominantly 'positively toned' (Wilson et al. 1989). These children had a high level of day-to-day involvement with their siblings, were aware of their siblings' special needs and felt strong feelings of responsibility towards their siblings. In addition, siblings also acknowledged sadness, anxiety and anger associated with their siblings and more than half of the children indicated that they would like to participate in some sort of support groups for siblings of children with disabilities.

Implications for working with families

It is clear from the above discussion that siblings tend to be personally well-adjusted and the sibling relationship can be close when a child in the family has a disability. Nevertheless siblings experience different challenges and sometimes more intense emotions – and from a younger age – than usual. Therefore, it can be helpful when those around them are sensitive to these extra challenges.

At the same time, you need to remember that all siblings experience ups and downs in their relationships and that maladjustment of one child may have nothing to do with the disability of another child in the family. You must also keep in mind that if you somehow encourage (often unwittingly) the child with the disability to be the main focus of the parents, you will inevitably affect others within the family, including siblings.

Siblings of children with disabilities want information about disabilities, opportunities to talk about feelings, time to hear about the experiences of other siblings, opportunities to meet with people with whom they can share their feelings of pride and joy and strategies to plan for the future (Cramer et al. 1997).

Information

Siblings need information about the cause of the disability, its prognosis, and special services their sister or brother will need – both now and in the future. They need to know also whether they themselves are vulnerable to the disability in any way, through genetics or by infection. The information needs to be balanced and honest (Powell and Gallagher 1993). It will need embellishment as the child grows older (Cramer et al. 1997). Seligman and Darling (1997) report that, for instance, children aged between six and nine years want to know what their brother or sister can and cannot do, and they want to know about speech and motor development; while older children (aged 10 to 12 years) tend to want information about the disabled child's future and their own chances of having a child with a disability.

It is important for parents to raise the topic with siblings to explain the child's disability, and to respond to the siblings' questions and fears. Siblings may not ask questions of their parents in order to protect them from talking about the disability or to protect the family from tension that arises when it is discussed.

Siblings will have private explanations of how come their brother or sister has a disability, and so adults need to ask the children what their understanding is (Seligman and Darling 1997). This allows confusions to be replaced by facts, and guilt about being the cause (often arising from young children's magical thinking) to be addressed. Parents can help children to cope with their sibling's disability by giving them some words to use to describe it and explain it to friends (Roe 1988).

Finally, siblings need information about how to deal with uncomfortable feelings about their sister or brother with the disability. It is also important that siblings are told that they do not have to look after other people all the time.

Throughout their lives, siblings will require frequent updates of information. Adults will need to check that the children understand what they have been told, and encourage them to talk and ask questions about the disability at any time.

Opportunities to talk

Although parents can help their children by accepting the children's feelings – even the 'ugly' ones – at times, parents will feel emotionally unavailable as a result of already having so many demands on them. In that case, it can help if they can organize someone else for their children to talk to – such as a family friend or relative.

Siblings benefit from the opportunity to talk about their feelings because it reduces the negative emotions and resentment which may obstruct their relationships with their siblings. With an opportunity to express the full range of emotions, the siblings can achieve four things, listed by Powell and Gallagher (1993):

- They can come to a greater understanding of emotions – such as anxiety – and the causes of their feelings.
- They can be guided to develop skills for coping and adjusting and to handle their feelings constructively. They can develop skills for handling conflicts that arise concerning the sibling's disability.
- They can receive permission to pursue their own growth and to have their own needs met. Younger siblings can have permission not to act as if they were older than the disabled child.
- With acceptance of their ambivalent feelings towards their disabled brother or sister, siblings will be freed up to act on the positive feelings that they experience, with the result that the sibling relationship can grow stronger. If the siblings are denied their 'negative' feelings, they will resent that fact and could come to resent the sibling.

Sibling support groups

Miller (1985, in Powell and Gallagher 1993) reports that siblings need to meet together, without professionals or parents, so that their feelings do not hurt their parents and are not criticized. Siblings do not need to hear the benefits of having a child with a disability in their family – because they already appreciate these benefits – but they need time out to speak about the personal costs with other people who can truly understand.

This is illustrated in a question and answer activity that was instituted by Cramer and colleagues (1997). When one child asked whether it was normal to feel embarrassed and want to run and hide when her sister had a seizure in public, other children whose own brothers or sisters had disabilities were able to reassure her that her feelings were natural and that it was okay to feel as she did. They suggested that she might need to work out some of her feelings with someone.

Counselling

For most siblings, informal support from the family will be enough for them to receive the support they need. For a few others, professional counselling might be beneficial. For this reason, Powell and Gallagher (1993) list some questions that professionals can ask siblings:

- How did you become aware of your sibling's disability?
- Has it meant extra responsibilities for you? If so, did you take these on voluntarily, or are you required to help?
- Do you think that family life has changed because of the sibling's disability?
- Do other people react differently to you when they learn you have a sister or brother with a disability?
- Has having a sibling with a disability affected your social life, friend-ships, future plans?
- Have you been included in plans made for your sibling?

Professionals can also help siblings to contemplate the future and to ask themselves how obliged they should feel to look after their disabled brother or sister (Seligman and Darling 1997). For some children, this will be a central issue so that they can grow up free of anxiety about their responsibility for their sibling and without guilt if they cannot meet the high expectations that are placed on them, either by their family or themselves. They might need encouragement to stay in balance and to let themselves appreciate their own childhood and cater to their own needs.

Family support from community services

A further important way to help siblings is to arrange regular respite care for the disabled child, so that the other family members can partici-pate in activities which otherwise they cannot do. Respite care alleviates some of the parents' workload, allows them to relax, gives them a chance to focus on their own needs, and allows them to attend to the needs of the siblings. In turn, siblings who worry about their parents will be relieved to see that the parents are looking after themselves and will be able to relax too.

Education

Many siblings want information about their sibling's disability and want to learn how to teach or respond to the behaviour of their sister or brother. This was demonstrated in a study of sibling interaction where siblings would have benefited from knowledge about how to communicate and modify activities to facilitate their play with their deaf-blind brothers and sisters (Heller et al. 1999).

Siblings may benefit from attending some planning sessions with the professionals who are involved in their sister's or brother's care. Like fathers of children with disabilities, siblings often lack this contact with professionals and so lack the opportunity to ask their own questions in this safe context.

It is well established that parents do not necessarily want to act as their child's teacher or therapist and that the same is true of siblings. Therefore while the care and education of family members with disabilities can be a family affair, it is probably useful to proceed with caution if planning to involve siblings formally in the delivery of an aspect of their brother's or sister's remedial programme.

Siblings in the classroom

If you have a student in your class who is the sibling of a child with a disability, you will need to consider whether that child has special needs associated with this. Developmentally, it is common for the sibling to have a similar disability to another family member's but for that to go undetected as it is less severe than the recognized disability. For instance, the siblings of children with autism often themselves have disordered or impaired language skills; as this seems minor compared to autism, it may not be detected.

Emotionally, the child may be preoccupied at times with the range of emotions and added responsibilities described in this chapter. It is important that teachers do not add to these challenges, especially when the siblings attend the same school. For example, siblings might be relied upon to relay messages to parents concerning the disabled brother or sister, or to attend to the child's needs at playtime. These responsibilities can be exacerbated when the family is of a non-English speaking background, and the non-disabled child in the family takes on the role of translating for teachers and parents at case conferences about his brother or sister. As these can be a frequent event, the burden on the young child can be overwhelming.

Implications for parents

Parents aim to consider the needs of all children in the family. This was evident in my (Susan's) study (McKenzie 1996) where parents mentioned their efforts to ensure that the child with the disability did not become the total focus of the family and that the needs of all children were met. Although a focus on the child with the disability is natural at times, particularly during medical crises or transitions between services, many parents try to limit the impact of this on their other children (McKenzie 1996). For example, they may ensure that they do not discuss the disabled child's difficulties in the hearing of siblings and make an effort to provide non-disabled siblings with extra attention to ensure they do not feel neglected because of any special attention that their sibling receives. Professionals can assist parents in this task by being aware of sibling needs and allowing their time out of home to be a respite from any additional responsibilities that they experience.

If parents need siblings to contribute to caring for their brother or sister with a disability, the parents still need to retain executive control of their family. They must decide what tasks need doing, and ask the brother or sister to help out, rather than expecting a child to become responsible for deciding what needs to be done.

Conclusion: Siblings

While the research tells us much about sibling relationships where one member has a disability, our information is still formative and so, when working with families, we need to approach all family members – including siblings – with a listening ear, rather than having preconceived notions about what they may be experiencing.

Lobato (1990) cautions us against attributing a sibling's difficulties to being raised with a sister or brother who has a disability as the difficulties may have occurred anyway. While it is easy to blame the obvious – a child's disability – for the difficulties that family members are experiencing, individuals are more complex than this and their emotions have many influences (Hayes 1998).

Grandparents

Family systems theory makes us aware that support from extended family members is integral to the adjustment of all family members (Seligman et al. 1997). As members of families' social networks, grandparents can have a significant influence on family functioning.

Grandparents are able to influence and support children in a way that no other relative can (Seligman and Darling 1997). The grandparent relationship is longer lasting now than in the past: the grandparent role can last for over half of the grandparent's life, and well into adulthood for the grandchild.

When they are emotionally supportive, grandparents enable parents to accept their child and provide models for the responses of siblings. With support from their own parents, fathers are likely to engage more actively with their disabled child and are better adjusted themselves, mothers feel more positively about the children, and the parents' marriage is strengthened (Sandler 1998; Seligman and Darling 1997).

Grandparents' emotional responses

Grandparents' emotional responses can be mixed. Some want to protect their own children from the 'burden' of the grandchild's disability, but this can take the form of refusing to acknowledge the grandchild's difficulties. Grandparents' attempts to allay the parents' fears can prolong the parents' anxiety and delay their procurement of appropriate services for their child (Bentley-Williams and Butterfield 1996). The grandparents' lack of appreciation of the grandchild's particular needs can cause parents to withdraw from discussing their concerns with the grandparents, and thus cause them to lose a potential source of support.

Some writers talk of grandparents' 'dual grief': one part being grief for their adult son or daughter whose child has been born with or acquired a disability, and a second part being grief on the grandchild's behalf as well.

Many people who become grandparents have had little contact themselves with people with disabilities. In their day, children with developmental disabilities might have been placed in institutions or special educational settings and were seldom seen in the community. Thus, grandparents' lack of contact with people with disabilities can mean that they lack information about disabilities, or that what information they do have is inaccurate.

If their understanding of the disability is incomplete, even with the best of intentions, grandparents might burden the disabled child's parents with 'unwanted, inaccurate, or outdated advice' about the child's needs (Meyer 1993: 89) or might question the necessity for specialist interventions. This can undermine the parents' confidence in their decisions for their child's care.

At other times, grandparents may accuse their son- or daughter-in-law of being at fault for giving their son or daughter a disabled child. Sometimes, they search their son- or daughter-in-law's family for genetic 'defects' in order to blame them for the disability. In such cases, although grandparents are part of the family's social network, they are not actually supportive and can hinder the family's adjustment (Sandler 1998).

On the other hand, grandparents have had a good deal of life experience and, in many cases, have observed others surviving – or themselves have overcome – many challenges in life. They may face the challenge of the grandchild's disability with equanimity, in the knowledge that this too is surmountable: life goes on.

Limitations on grandparents' availability

Grandparents and parents may not be available to support each other at a time when both need support very much, and when the siblings need guidance about how to respond. If grandparents are having difficulties in coming to terms with disability in their grandchildren, they might not be able to offer support to the child's parents as they need support themselves (Sandler 1998).

The grandparent role can be limited by the wishes of the child's parents. Therefore this may make relationships or the act of caring for grandchildren more precious as it is dependent on parents' approval and willingness to allow it to continue.

Grandparents' availability may be affected by changes in family life. One such change is the geographical mobility of families. Some grandparents may simply live too far away to be of practical help; however, for those who are nearby but unsupportive, their geographical closeness may lead to more rather than less stress for the parents (Seligman et al. 1997).

A second change is in the role of grandparents. Now, instead of being elderly and available, many grandparents are still vital people with full-time occupations of their own. Their own full-time employment may mean that, while they are able to offer emotional support and warmth to their grandchild and family, they are actually less available than in the past to provide intensive or practical support.

Some grandparents make themselves unavailable for supportive functions such as baby-sitting out of a lack of confidence in their ability to look after their disabled grandchild. If as a result, they are willing to baby-sit the non-disabled children but not the child who has a disability, such apparent favouritism is likely to hurt and alienate the parents, and send signals of unacceptance to the child and siblings.

Forms of support provided by grandparents

Grandparents are able to provide both instrumental support and emotional support to families. For example, they provide instrumental support when they baby-sit, provide respite or regular care of the children, provide families with financial assistance or assist with household chores.

Emotional support may take the form of a listening ear or non-judge-mental advice, acceptance of child's disability and affirmation of the parents' ability to cope (Mirfin-Veitch et al. 1997).

Despite restrictions in the availability of some grandparents, increasing numbers of grandparents (usually grandmothers) are contributing actively to the daily care of their young grandchildren (Baydar and Brookes-Gunn 1998). Grandmothers reveal that this role is very intense and emotionally complex, affecting their relationships with all family members and causing them to re-experience their own parenting history, with some resenting having to resume a role that they thought was already fulfilled (Gattai and Musatti 1998; Seligman et al. 1997). The grandparenting role provides a repetition of motherhood and allows for critical self-reflection, thereby providing an opportunity for grandparents to change their caretaking behaviours (Gattai and Musatti 1998).

Implications for working with families

There are two rationales for providing support to grandparents of children with disabilities: first, they can have their own needs for informa-tion and emotional support (Meyer 1993); second, they are often in a position to provide support and practical assistance to the family, as long as they are knowledgeable and confident about doing so.

With the parents' permission, you could invite grandparents to programme-planning sessions. This allows the grandparents to hear infor-mation about their grandchild and the disability first-hand, which is likely to increase their confidence in their ability to make a contribution, however informal.

It can also benefit grandparents to have a forum where they can discuss their feelings and needs. This is especially important when they offer significant care for their grandchildren (Bell and Smith 1996; Meyer 1993). At the school level, coffee mornings or other welcoming activities for grandparents will not only acknowledge and celebrate their involvement in their grandchildren's lives, but also provide a venue where they can support each other.

Summary

Both siblings and grandparents have their own personal needs arising from their relationship with their sibling or grandchild who has a disability. Grandparents can offer parents child care advice – and, sometimes practical caregiving help – and can share coping strategies that worked for them in the past. Through their community links, they can help parents to gain access to community services. The emotional support that they can offer can be a source of great strength and comfort to all of the immediate family. The implications for professionals are clear: we need to empower grandparents to provide this support, both for the sake of their grandchildren and the children's parents, and also for their own emotional wellbeing. Meanwhile, for siblings, we need to be careful how much responsibility we encourage such young people to accept, lest they become overwhelmed and subordinate their own needs to those of others.

Discussion questions

1. In your professional role, what can you do to support a child whose brother or sister has a disability?
2. Within your service, are there any opportunities to provide formal supports for children whose brother or sister has a disability?
3. How can you involve extended family members in a child's programme?

Chapter 6
Families' service needs

The foresighted professional person knows that it is the parent who truly bears the responsibility for the child, and the parent cannot be replaced by episodic professional service.

Hobbs (1975: 228–9, in Dunst et al. 1988: 8)

Key points

- The services that families may require will change throughout their life.
- Lack of services, the inappropriateness of services, and the families' competing demands can affect their utilization of services.
- Although most professionals will assume that more services are beneficial to families, there are occasions when a multitude of services can overwhelm parents, in which case fewer services would actually be more helpful.

Introduction

Needs arise from circumstances both within and outside of the family (Dunst et al. 1988). They are relative, and are unique to individual families. They arise when:

- parents perceive that they are experiencing concerns or difficulties;
- they recognize that there are other options – that there is a discrepancy between their present circumstances and how things could be;
- they know about some resources that could assist them;
- they are willing to use these to arrive at a solution (Dunst et al. 1988).

Sometimes, families might appear to us to be needy yet are making no attempt to solve their problem, as we see it. This may come about because they believe that they do not have the necessary resources for overcoming the problem. In that case, they might be aware of the difficulties they are having but do not seek help as they cannot foresee being able to use it. They do not see any potential benefits of attempting to solve their difficulty and so feel stuck. Thus, part of your assessment of the family's needs will be also to examine what resource limitations might be blocking their commitment to solving their problems (Dunst et al. 1988).

Needs assessment

In the context of assessing what services families could find useful, the word *need* conjures up some sort of deficiency. But it is safe to assume that parents know even more than they are showing us, in which case the notion of personal deficiencies is not useful. For that reason, like Dunst and colleagues (1988, 1994), we prefer the terms *goals* or *aspirations*, rather than *needs*, as the former terms imply that we focus on the parents' wishes for their child. They will be motivated to work on their own goals more than they will be to work on our agenda and, therefore, it is our job to further the parents' goals.

This focus on goals changes assessment from its focus on identifying and ameliorating families' deficiencies – or even from identifying and building on their strengths – to listening to what the family says that it needs, not judging for them what they require (Dunst et al. 1988, 1994; Sokoly and Dokecki 1995). It is time to move beyond the paternalistic assumption that we can assess parents' wants and needs better than they can themselves. Yes, we will be aware of the skills that they bring to the care and education of their children, and we can apprise them of the services that might be useful to them, but it is not our job to change their agenda so that it matches our own. We have to work with what they give us.

Abandoning professional dominance is a safe option as parents seldom deliberately set out to limit their child's development or harm their child: they want what is best for their child. So do you. We realize that sometimes you may disagree about how to go about achieving that best outcome, but that arguing for your point of view will make the family even more resistant to your suggestions.

Factors affecting families' access to and participation in services

Parents of young children are more likely to receive the types of support they need than are parents of adolescents (Baxter 1987; Westling 1996). Westling, for example, reports that 90% of parents of preschoolers with disabilities said that they did not need any services other than those they were receiving; whereas Smith (1997) found that by the time the children became adults, over half of their (now elderly) parents used services such as day programmes, welfare payments, transportation, and recreational activities, but fewer than a third used other services such as case management, support groups, respite care or specialized therapies.

When parents fail to use services, this is sometimes incorrectly attributed to lack of interest and motivation on their part, rather than to the possibility that the services do not satisfy their needs. Sometimes, parents are accused of 'shopping behaviour' which means that they go from one professional to another in a series of attempts to find help. Especially when the treatments that they seek are unorthodox, 'shopping' is often attributed to the parents' 'denial' of their child's needs and to their misplaced optimism about finding a 'cure'. However, many parents have told us that this 'shopping', particularly their recourse to unorthodox services, is based on acceptance, not denial: they are well aware that unorthodox treatments have limited potential benefits for their child but ask that we respect their search for something that may help. They also tell us that they hear the mainstream practitioners' criticisms that unorthodox methods are 'unscientific', but that the conventional specialists cannot recommend what else they might do. The end result is advice to do nothing. And they cannot do that.

Thus, the obvious inference from their 'shopping' for services is that present services are not supplying what they need. Parents will continue their search until they find a service that does offer the support that they require.

The following factors can limit parents' access to suitable services:

- Parents of lower occupational status are less likely to be informed of service options (Baxter 1989).
- Parents' personal schooling history may make them hostile to or in awe of teachers and so they do not seek to become involved in their child's education (Lovitt and Cushing 1999).
- The family's internal commitments may mean that they are not available emotionally or physically for engaging with service personnel – for instance, something as mundane as full-time or shift work can make attending meetings impossible (Bright and Wright 1986; Lovitt and Cushing 1999).
- Some parents feel that they cannot meet the high expectations for their involvement (Mori 1983).
- Language barriers may restrict knowledge of services by people with reading difficulties or for whom English is not their first language (Garrick 1986).

- Migrants' feelings of powerlessness and inferiority may make them uneasy when consulting professionals (Bennett 1988; Smith and Ryan 1987).
- Previous intensive involvement may have burnt out parents or disillusioned them about the possibility that any new service can achieve significant change for their child or family;
- Some children with special needs do not want their parents to become involved with their schooling hassles (Lovitt and Cushing 1999), just as is the case for non-disabled children.

Parents may decline to utilize a service because what we are recommending does not meet their needs. For example, I (Louise) once worked with parents who were trying to cooperate with the speech therapy programme that was teaching their child 'ing' endings to words, as that was the next developmental stage for the child to achieve. However, this family's most pressing need was for their five-year-old child to be toilet trained so that she could attend preschool and then school. It was not that they did not value the speech pathologist or her ideas, but they did not *need* their daughter to be learning 'ing' endings just now, especially as she could make her meaning clear even when her sentences were not grammatically correct.

Families' service needs

Throughout this book we have repeatedly emphasized that families vary in their internal and external resources and supports, their goals for their children, and their culture. This means that different families will have different needs or aspirations for their children. Furthermore, those needs will change over time and according to their child's development.

When parents of children with disabilities are asked about the professional support that they have received, many indicate that they need more support than they presently receive (Baxter 1987; Mahoney et al. 1990; Williams and Roper 1985). However, this is less the case within the education system, where most parents report being satisfied with their child's schooling, especially in inclusive settings (Westling 1996; Westling and Plaute 1999).

Aside from educational services, parents require a range of support from information, to respite care, and opportunities to meet their own social needs (Bailey et al. 1992).

Information

Parents' first need is for information. As we discussed in Chapter 3, this and other needs will change through the years. At first, they may require assistance to understand their own and other family members' emotional reactions to their child's disability; sooner or later they will need information about their child's condition and likely prognosis; they will need information about the sorts of services that are available; and they might need some specific guidance about how to respond to their child's special needs (Hayes 1998). Others will have very practical concerns about their eligibility for any social security benefits that could help offset any additional costs, about the availability of home help or respite services, or how to transport their child to specialist services or accommodate their child's special equipment.

When delivering information to parents, it is not up to us to assume that they *need* training in how to bring up their children. However, some might appreciate the chance to discuss issues relating to their children, either with other parents, with staff members or with a specialist whom you invite to deliver a session on a topic which the parents have nominated. Topics that tend to be of interest to parents are listed in the following box.

Information sought by parents

Parents tend to want information about:
- their child's disability;
- their child's learning characteristics and potential;
- how to teach the child at home;
- how to play with the child at home;
- their child's medical conditions;
- typical and atypical child development;
- range of available services;
- behaviour management strategies;
- parent support groups.

Source: adapted from Westling and Plaute (1999).

Once a child's programme is ongoing, parents most frequently want information about how their child is progressing (Westling 1996). This can be a delicate issue, as you must convey that the child is continuing to learn while not implying that the child's skills are approaching the normal range if they are not. We find it useful to say something such as, 'James is communicating more clearly now, and uses a number of words. This is obviously a big advance on earlier in the year, when he was not speaking at all. His skills then were below the one-year level. Now they are closer to the two-year level' (say, when James is aged four).

The second type of information that parents require is about services (Westling 1996), particularly at times of transition so that they can evaluate which service or school is most likely to meet their child's future needs.

Respite care

Respite care is one of the most requested services for families, especially when the children have behavioural difficulties (Hayes 1998; Nitschke 1994; Rimmerman et al. 1989). Yet, despite a high need for respite care being acknowledged by both families and professionals, only 30% of families in one study used formal respite care services (Salisbury 1990). In this case, it was found that parents chose to use other sources of respite from within their informal social networks.

The use of respite care increases mothers' feelings of wellbeing and, as a result, has positive effects for the functioning of families as a whole (Botuck and Winsberg 1991). As well as benefiting families, regular and planned use of respite care supports families to keep their children at home (Szwarc 1987). Without respite, it might prove too difficult for many families to maintain their primary caretaking role. However, it is only an interlude that is not a magic cure and so needs to be supplemented by in-home support for those families who are experiencing high stress levels (Hayes 1998).

In our experience, the shortage of respite care, and parents' own determination to look after their child themselves, means that some use respite services only in crises or when they are completely exhausted. This seems a pity: respite care is seen as an admission of failure, rather than as a proactive step to maintain the wellbeing of all family members. Although many parents say that they feel guilty about abandoning their child into care, particularly as they do not do this for their child or children without disabilities, you might like to point out that there are more opportunities for natural respite for their non-disabled children – say, when these children have sleep-overs at friends' places. Furthermore, sometimes, relatives are confident about baby-sitting the non-disabled children but feel less able to take care of a child with high medical needs and so natural respite in the form of baby-sitters may be less available for such children, in which case parents need alternative formal support.

In the early childhood years, child care centres are increasingly used by parents of non-disabled children, especially for children over the age of three years (Warfield and Hauser-Cram 1996). As was documented in Chapter 2, centre-based care has been shown to have beneficial effects for all areas of children's development, as long as the care is of high quality. Centre-based care also offers parents some natural respite.

However, relatively little is known about the suitability of centre-based care for children with special needs. In my research, I (Louise) (Porter 1999) noted that, although qualified to work with children without disabilities, caregivers had varying levels of awareness of special needs in their young charges, and minimal knowledge of what those special needs implied for programming. Furthermore, in the absence of sufficient support for inclusion, teachers and caregivers report having little confidence in their ability to cater adequately for children with disabilities (MacMullin and Napper 1993).

Child care can be inaccessible to many parents because of its cost, limited hours, and distance from the centre to home or work (Warfield and Hauser-Cram 1996). A child's special needs – particularly behavioural problems – can exacerbate accessibility problems as some centres will refuse to enrol the child, perhaps because of the mismatch between the child's needs and the centre's own characteristics which make meeting those needs difficult (Warfield and Hauser-Cram 1996).

Assessment

Another service that parents require is for their child to receive a comprehensive assessment so that service providers can plan for the child's particular needs. Special educators need a wide variety of information about their students (McLoughlin and Lewis 1994). To that end, parents want assessment to include more than norm-referenced tests, so that their child's daily living skills can be demonstrated (Ryndak et al. 1996). Parents believe that reliance on normed tests results in a focus on what their child *cannot* do, rather than on what skills he or she has, and perpetuates a curriculum based on readiness (or lack of it) rather than the teaching of ecologically valid skills.

This view was poignantly stated by some parents in my (Susan's) study (McKenzie 1993). They were distressed that assessment was carried out hurriedly in unfamiliar settings and felt that this gave their children little opportunity to perform to the best of their abilities. One parent reported: 'There was no attempt to find out what this kid can really do. It is a bit upsetting for me as a parent to see your kid labelled as "a dummy" when you know the potential' (McKenzie 1993: 60). Thereafter, the resulting underestimations can dictate professionals' perception of the children's abilities for many years to come.

Rowe (1990: 544) acknowledges this in her assertion that some professionals rely on assessments 'like a drunk might depend on a lamp-post – for support rather than illumination'. The message is clear: assessment involves more than testing alone. It requires that educators use a range of assessment measures (including criterion-based instruments, interviews with parents, behavioural observations and normed tests) to gain the fullest possible understanding of children's abilities and educational needs.

Part of your role in giving parents information about their child's disability and needs can be interpreting other professionals' reports for them. This will involve knowledge of disciplines other than your own and a close working relationship with other members of a multi-disciplinary team so that they can teach you some of the jargon in their specialty fields.

Notwithstanding the sometimes negative effects of labels on the individuals who receive them, diagnostic labels that arise from assessment can be useful to families, by describing, explaining and – at times – predicting the developmental progress of their child.

Description

A label can cluster together an otherwise confusing array of symptoms into a single known entity. Attention-deficit hyperactivity disorder (ADHD), for instance, groups together a cluster of inattentive, impulsive and over-active behaviours which otherwise would seem incomprehensible. The danger, however, with descriptive labels such as ADHD is that they can be misinterpreted as explanations.

Explanation

A label can explain why a child has particular impairments. For instance, a child with Down syndrome frequently has some heart anomalies. Two apparently unrelated problems can be subsumed under the one explanatory label. The danger with explanatory labels, of course, is allowing them to excuse a person from taking what steps may be possible to overcome some of the limitations which his or her impairment has caused.

Prognosis

A label can give parents some idea of the expected progress of a child's condition throughout life. The obvious danger with prognoses, however, is our incomplete knowledge which can cause us to under-estimate a child's potential.

Education

Education is a major service that parents require for their children. Three issues surface about parents' desires for their children's education: how much say they want to have in their children's education, what they want the children to learn, and where they want them to learn it (placement).

Parental choice

Westling (1996) reports that 80% of parents want power to choose the educational placements for their son or daughter and to contribute to educational planning for their children. Around the same proportion of parents report being satisfied with their level of involvement, regardless of what that level is (Westling 1996). Parents with high education are most likely to want to be involved, and most likely to achieve that (Freeman et al. 1999; Westling 1996; Westling and Plaute 1999).

Learning goals

On the whole, parents want teaching staff to listen to their curricular suggestions without becoming defensive (Ryndak et al. 1997). Parents' instructional goals for their children vary as the children get older and according to the severity of their disability (Westling 1996). In the preschool years parents emphasize motor, communication, and toileting skills; by middle childhood they focus on self-help skills and again on communication skills. Leisure and work skills figure in parents' wishes later. For children with severe disabilities, parents tend to be most interested in fostering social development; for those with milder disabilities, parents rate functional skills, academic skills, and then social skills as important goals (Westling 1996).

Above all, parents want their child's curriculum to be individualized and challenging, with specialist services provided, although not necessarily in a withdrawal situation but in the inclusive setting (Hodapp et al. 1998; Ryndak et al. 1996). They want their teachers to know about disability in general and individual children's specific disabilities and the impact of these on the children's development (Hodapp et al. 1998).

Placement

Parents' educational goals make a difference to their placement choices for their children. They have varying views on the ideal educational placement for their children who have disabilities, often depending on their child's needs, placement history and the parents' assessment of the ability of the regular class to meet their child's additional needs (Palmer et al. 1998a, 1998b; Westling 1996). Some find the convenience of their local school attractive (Freeman et al. 1999), while others favour inclusive educational settings largely for the positive role models in general classrooms and, in the case of less severely disabled children, for the extra educational challenge (Freeman et al. 1999; Hodapp et al. 1998; Ryndak et al. 1996). Even so, parents tend to realize that co-location alone is insufficient for friendships to develop and so want teachers to take active steps to facilitate friendships between children with and without disabilities (Palmer et al. 1998a; Ryndak et al. 1996).

Other parents feel that their children's educational needs are best met in segregated settings (Palmer et al. 1998a, 1998b; Ryndak et al. 1996); some prefer these because they are concerned for their child's physical and emotional safety in inclusive settings (Westling 1996); some want their son or daughter to be educated alongside children who have special needs on the grounds that these children are more 'forgiving and accepting' (Hodapp et al. 1998). Nevertheless, although many parents fear that inclusive settings may be less accepting of their children's special needs, children who do attend regular schools generally do not experience any such problems (Westling 1996) or, if problems do arise, these tend to diminish over time (Freeman et al. 1999).

Extracurricular activities

A further need of parents is for their children to be able to participate in extracurricular activities. Skills which children and young people learn in the community can benefit their academic performance at school (Johnson et al. 1997). However, many young people with disabilities know little about community-based leisure activities in which they could participate. School or other service personnel can promote their involvement in recreational pursuits by exploring their interests and then helping them to locate an activity in which they are interested and which has a successful record of inclusion (Bennett et al. 1998; Johnson et al. 1997). When parents and professionals allow children and young people with disabilities to determine for themselves the activities in which they would like to participate, their performance can exceed expectations, both in the leisure activity and in transferring into the classroom the skills that they have acquired elsewhere.

Informal social support

Many of the above needs apply to services that parents require for their children; in addition, the parents themselves have a need for support, both formal and informal. Caregivers who have a high level of contact with friends and relatives tend to have higher morale and feel less burdened than those with a lower level of such support (Greenberg et al. 1997). Parents with their own informal networks may not need any additional formal support. On the other hand, sometimes families and friends burden parents with their own distress about their young relative's disability, in which case formal support can be beneficial.

When parents have sufficient informal support, all that you may have to do is ensure that you do not undermine this (Dunst et al. 1988). Families need informal support permanently, whereas they require formal (professional) support only episodically – so you must ensure that they remain in touch with their informal support network. This could mean, for instance, ensuring that your recommendations do not demand so much of their time that they have none left over in which to maintain contact with extended family and friends.

Support groups

Some parents will benefit when your programme aims not only to meet their child's needs but also satisfies some of the parents' own social needs as well. Contact with other parents who attend your school or use your service can help some parents to feel less isolated. Formal support groups can offer mutual aid to their members, allow them to share information, and give participants an opportunity to express their emotions (Frank et al. 1996). They can be particularly useful in the early days subsequent to recognition of a child's disability, or when the particular disability is uncommon and parents need to exchange information about it (Greenberg et al. 1997).

Not all support groups are helpful, however. Some parents of children with disabilities can be reluctant to join a programme for children with similar disabilities, as they find it too confronting to see their child as part of such a group. Furthermore, when parents are pessimistic about their child's future, socializing with other caregivers of children with similar disabilities can actually amplify rather than reduce their concerns (Greenberg et al. 1997). This might be because all group members might need support themselves and so actually add to the demands on each other (Greenberg et al. 1997).

Some will want to meet other parents whose child shares their child's disability; some want to adjust in private. Those who want to take one day at a time can find it too confronting to have contact with older children with the same disability as their own child's. One parent recounted to me (Louise) how she had been visited in hospital by a mother and adolescent with Down syndrome the day after the birth of her child with that disability. Although they visited with the best of intentions of being there to answer her questions, the new parent was not ready yet to talk about her child's disability and was considerably distressed to have to face the long-term future so soon after the child's birth. Parents of non-disabled children are not confronted so soon after their child's birth with statistics about the likelihood that the child will use illegal drugs, become a delinquent, drink and drive, or have difficulties finding work upon leaving school, but we expect parents of children with disabilities to be ready to hear about all their child's potential problems as soon as they know of his or her disability.

Support groups are different from parent training groups. In parent training groups, there is an agenda for teaching parents specific skills relating to their child who has a disability. In support groups, the parents set their own agenda of providing mutual support and sharing experiences with others who are in similar circumstances to themselves. The message, however, is that such groups should not supplant parents' natural support networks or add to their distress.

Advocacy

Yet another service that parents can require from time to time is support to advocate for services to meet their child's or their own needs. Advocacy involves working to bring about social change to remove barriers to effective services for children and their families (Seligman and Darling 1997). Although parents can normally be their own advocates, there are times when professionals may have to be active in advocating for particular services for a child and family (Seligman and Darling 1997). This might involve addressing the social constraints on effective service – including physical barriers to community access, cultural barriers such as prejudice, and social barriers such as a lack of appropriate services (Seligman and Darling 1997). Advocacy can occur at a range of levels (Rosin et al. 1996):

- governmental advocacy, in which parent groups – perhaps with professional support – advocate for legislative changes to meet the needs of individuals with disability;
- organizational advocacy, in which a professional who is outside a system acts as a broker for services for the family, helping them to negotiate the service system;
- internal advocacy, in which the professional from within the system advocates for the family's and child's needs. An internal advocate will have more knowledge of the services than an external one, but at the same time could be tied to the political culture of the organization and might not be able to influence the systems of which he or she is a part;
- supporting parents to advocate on their own and their child's behalf.

Transition planning

In Chapter 3, we described that the times when parents and their children are likeliest to be stressed are when they are moving from one service to another or from one life stage to another, such as from preschool to primary school, or from school to employment. At such times, parents mainly want their new service providers and teachers to find out as early as possible about their child's unique needs (Lovitt and Cushing 1999). Thus, it is important to listen to what the family wants from the next service that they and their son or daughter are entering. Hutchins and Renzaglia (1998) suggest that when involved in planning transitions with parents and young people, you ask questions such as:

- What do you want your child to achieve in this new setting?
- What experiences has the young person had that could prepare him or her for, or could be useful in, the new setting?
- What does your child most enjoy doing?
- What sort of assistance and supports will your child need in the new setting?
- How does he or she communicate with others?
- In what ways do you (the parents) want to become involved in the new setting?
- What sort of feedback do you need, (a) in the initial days, and (b) subsequently, about how your child is settling in and performing here?

In order to help plan for the young person's next placement, you will need a long-term perspective on the family's concerns and involvement to date. It will also be important to involve the children in planning for their future, especially as they reach adolescence.

As you gather the parents' and young people's answers to such questions, it will be important to be clear with them if something that they want is not available. It does not benefit them if you promise something that you subsequently cannot deliver. Part of your joint planning, then, might be to develop a plan for surmounting gaps in services.

Counselling

Another service which parents might require is counselling. However, like Seligman and Darling (1997), we caution against assuming that families with a disabled child will necessarily need counselling – any more than would other families. This point is reinforced by two separate meanings of the term *counselling*. Sometimes, counselling refers to providing information and at other times the term is used to refer to the provision of emotional support. We may be safe to assume that parents with a child with a disability will require different information about their child's atypical needs compared with other parents, but this does not necessarily mean that they will need more emotional support – in the form of counselling – than other families.

Counselling involves helping people to use their present skills to make effective choices in their lives and to act on these (Benjamin 1969, in Shertzer and Stone 1974; Nelson-Jones 1988; Rogers, in Avila et al. 1977). It does not involve convincing them of what they should do, but allowing them to discover for themselves which solutions fit for them (Geldard 1998; Stewart 1986).

The counsellor who is supporting parents of a child with disabilities may need to adopt a variety of roles with respect to the services already described in this chapter: helping parents to gather information; assisting their access to services; interpreting assessments; acting as a sounding board, ally or advocate; supporting their decisions. In performing these roles, a counsellor should not try to minimize the severity of the child's condition or the parents' feelings about it, but must accept – rather than try to 'cure' – the feelings that parents may be experiencing.

As described in Chapter 4, there are three ways of adjusting to stress: solving the problem that is provoking the stress reaction; changing how you feel about it; or learning to live with circumstances that cannot be changed (Compas 1987). Problem solving works best when people feel that they have some control over the problem; while emotion-focused coping and behavioural adjustment are most appropriate when they cannot change their circumstances (Greenberg et al. 1997; Spirito et al. 1991). Thus, counselling will involve helping parents to see whether they can control the problem and, if so, to take steps to solve it; and, if not, to find ways to adjust to it. When it comes to coping, it does not actually matter which skills individuals use to manage their stress, but that they do *something* productive (Rutter 1985). Therefore, there will seldom be a need to teach parents new coping skills but simply to identify which ones they are presently using and encourage them to expand on those (Ryan 1989).

Referring on

One important service that professionals must be able to offer families is referral to another practitioner. No professional knows everything there is to know in a given field. Professionals who are working with families with a child who has a disability need to recognize when they cannot meet the family's needs and, in such cases, plan how to refer the family to someone who can. This involves being aware of the range of services that could potentially be useful to families, and knowing how to refer families to these services. It can also require interpersonal skills to facilitate the family's acceptance of the referral.

Coordination of services

The final need of parents is for some coordination of the services that they are using. The push towards privatization of social services, towards a 'user pays' mentality of service use, and the use of generic services for special populations together mean that services are now more fragmented than ever for children and youth with special needs. Where once specialists such as psychologists and speech pathologists may have worked for an agency designated to serve this population, nowadays many of these agencies have been disbanded and services 'outsourced' to private practitioners. However, these private practitioners may no longer have specialized knowledge in the disability field but instead serve individuals with a whole range of needs. Although these trends have their potential benefits, one cost is that there is no single agency that is responsible for serving the needs of young people with disabilities, making it difficult for their parents to locate appropriate services (Hughes and May 1988).

A lack of service coordination is especially common when the nature of their child's disability is uncertain. In some cases, it ultimately turns out that the disability falls outside the criteria for admission to a particular service, and so the parents' search is in vain, unless they can locate and afford alternative private practitioners.

Faced with such difficulties, many parents find a case manager to be an asset in helping them to negotiate a complex service system, especially when their child has multiple needs (Westling 1996; Westling and Plaute 1999). Others, however, want to assume this role for themselves so that they retain control of their own circumstances (Dunst et al. 1988). The implication, clearly, is that professionals need to ask parents about their preferences.

Needs of parents with disabilities

For adults with intellectual (or learning) disabilities, having a family may be their first real experience of ordinary family life, intimacy and family love (Booth and Booth 1995). When their children attend school, there is a network of other parents to meet, and so their own inclusion in the community can be enhanced. Thus, as with non-disabled parents, parents with disabilities gain tremendous satisfaction from their parenting role.

However, adults with intellectual disabilities are more likely to be unemployed, living in poverty, and lacking in informal social support (Feldman 1994; Llewellyn 1990, 1994). Although they are unlikely to have children with congenital disabilities (Whitman et al. 1987), as a result of the poverty that characterizes this population, the children are at risk of neglect and of receiving insufficient stimulation, with consequent impairment in their development, especially past the age of three years (Llewellyn 1990; Schilling et al. 1982; Tymchuk 1992). As poverty tends to be long term, the risk to the children is prolonged.

Another risk factor for parents with intellectual disabilities is the quality of the parenting which they received as children. Those who were in institutions as children will have received little parental care themselves and thus will have acquired few parenting skills, with the result that they may be overly controlling in their parenting style (Llewellyn 1990; Tymchuk 1992). Meanwhile, those reared at home may not have been entrusted with the supervision of children (Schilling et al. 1982) and so they too will lack experience with and knowledge of children and their development.

Despite these risks of impoverished living circumstances and poor parenting role models, the majority of parents with mild intellectual (learning) disabilities are able to parent adequately (Llewellyn 1990). Recent studies show that the parenting skills of those with intellectual disability can be similar to those of non-disabled parents of similar socioeconomic status (Tymchuk 1992). This is especially so when there are two parents and fewer children in the family.

When the risk factors are present, these parents are unlikely to succeed in their parenting role without extensive assistance (Booth and Booth 1995). Services will need to be preventive rather than crisis-oriented (Llewellyn et al. 1999a), without, however, burdening parents with help that they do not need. As with any parents, these parents need to feel empowered by their relationships with their professional advisers so more time must be taken to determine what services they want (McConnell et al. 1997).

The following training and support needs have been identified for this population of parents (Llewellyn et al. 1999a; McConnell et al. 1997):

- parenting skills;
- living skills;
- self-esteem and assertiveness skills;
- social skills;
- access to mainstream services;
- advocacy.

An additional need is for professionals to support the children, particularly those who are taking on adult roles at a young age to compensate for their parents' inabilities.

Parenting skills

Parents who have intellectual or learning disabilities may need support to keep their children safe and to respond appropriately to the children's changing needs as they develop. Parents with intellectual (learning) disabilities have been shown to profit from training in basic child care tasks to do with the children's health and hygiene (Feldman et al. 1992). Such training in basic skills may need to be topped up as the children develop – for instance, by teaching the parents how to toilet train their toddler (Greene et al. 1995).

This training needs to be at the skill (performance) level as well as at the knowledge level, and must give parents opportunities to perform new skills at home rather than in a clinic setting (Bakken et al. 1993; Booth and Booth 1995; Fantuzzo et al. 1986; Feldman 1994; McConnell et al. 1997). These parents tend to need actual demonstrations of a skill that they are learning, but verbal instruction is sufficient to help them maintain a skill that is already in their repertoire (Feldman et al. 1989).

The main developmental concern for children whose parents have intellectual (learning) disabilities is the children's language delays. Feldman and colleagues (1986) were highly successful in teaching these parents how to respond to their children's vocalizations, with resulting dramatic improvement in the children's language skills.

The increasing disparity between the parents' and their children's intellectual skills as the children age can intensify parent-child conflicts, while the parents' concrete thinking, decision-making and limited communication skills can result in impulsive or inflexible approaches to solving such problems (Llewellyn 1990; Llewellyn and Brigden 1995; Schilling et al. 1982). They may need training in non-aggressive means of child behaviour management and positive parent-child interaction skills.

Some studies – mainly those in the early childhood years – have accused this population of parents of being unresponsive to their children. When this is so, they benefit from training in observing and responding to their children's cues (Feldman et al. 1986, 1989). But many parents evidence great pride in their children's achievements and are responsive to the children's changing needs (Booth and Booth 1995), in which case such training is unnecessary.

Living skills

Their impoverished living circumstances make knowing how to budget a high priority for parents with intellectual disabilities. In order to care adequately for their children, they might need additional training in tasks such as housekeeping and shopping (McConnell et al. 1997).

Self-esteem and assertiveness

Parents with an intellectual disability are frequently in perpetual fear of having their children removed from them and so are unlikely to resist interference in their lives or to report problems they are having, in case these become a catalyst for removal of the children (Booth and Booth 1995). They may need support to be assertive, (a) to decline services that they do not want, and (b) to ask for services that they do require.

Social support

Parents with intellectual disabilities have high needs for support, which can overtax their informal networks with the result that these parents are frequently socially isolated (Booth and Booth 1995). On the other hand, many parents experience the concern of relatives as intrusive and so do not want to encourage them to give unsolicited advice (Llewellyn 1995). To enable them to maintain links with the community and thus expand their informal support network, they might need training in social interaction and conflict resolution skills (Fantuzzo et al. 1986). Meanwhile, they need to know that they can call on professional advice as a backup (Llewellyn 1995).

Access to services

Professionals may have to be more active in providing practical support such as arranging transport to appointments, and helping parents with intellectual disabilities to apply for social welfare benefits or other services (Llewellyn et al. 1999a). Professionals will need to spend more time providing information about available services to parents who have intellectual disabilities. Mainstream services may be too complex for them to participate in, while training sessions in groups with non-disabled parents may expose parents with disabilities to ridicule and impatience from other group members (Llewellyn 1994, Llewellyn and Brigden 1995), so generic services will need to be carefully screened for their receptivity to parents with disabilities.

Advocacy within the service system

Poorly coordinated services can lead to contradictory and confusing advice to parents who have intellectual disabilities (McConnell et al. 1997). Meanwhile, impractical advice and lack of continuity of service is a particular problem for them.

Moreover, these parents are often exposed to system abuse in which they are subjected to unfair degrees of scrutiny, are treated as children despite being responsible parents, are obliged to accept services that they do not want, and have their actions and decisions undermined by those who are supposed to be helping them (Booth and Booth 1995; McConnell et al. 1997). This makes it crucial that they have a case manager or similar professional who can advocate for their needs within the service system.

Support for the children

In a poignant account of growing up with a mother with an intellectual disability and a psychotic father, Ronai (1997) reminds professionals that the children need to be allowed to talk about their experiences. Forcing them to pretend that their family is 'normal' adds another layer of abuse to the challenges of looking after parents while one is still a child.

Implications for service providers

The implication for educators is that when you have a child in your class whose parents have an intellectual (learning) disability, you need to relate to those parents with the same courtesy as you do to any parents, but provide your information in very concrete terms, bearing in mind their reading and vocabulary skills. You will need to take heed of these parents' difficulties with understanding and learning new concepts (Llewellyn 1995). When you focus on what they want to know and learn, you will motivate them to continue to consult you (Llewellyn and Brigden 1995).

You are in an ideal position to refer the family to suitable agencies that could help them, as long as you have their permission to do so. (The exception would be instances of child neglect or abuse, in which case their consent is not required.) To avoid confusion and frustration for the parents, if they are consulting other professionals, you will need to take extra steps to ensure that your advice coincides with that of other workers (Llewellyn 1995).

Rural services

Families in rural areas have been identified as being in need of more adequate services; the equity in service provision is impaired by their geographic isolation. Services in small towns and country regions are scarce in all fields, including the disability area. Distances between children mean that it is difficult to work with small groups of children with disabilities, and parents are denied the social support provided by other parents in similar circumstances to their own. Nevertheless, they do experience satisfaction with the social networks that they do have (Minnes et al. 1989).

Transport is a major problem, both for families and professionals. Their distance from others may mean that the parents are the child's only resource, while at the same time, the family is likely to be at least as busy as city families. Another difficulty in rural areas is the high turnover of specialist professionals.

Because of a lack of formal services, many rural families choose to relocate to the city. This means that the parents must secure new employment (if either parent *can* gain paid employment), a new home, appropriate services for their child, and a new school for the children. These many changes must be managed at the same time as the family has been severed from the informal social supports formerly available in their home town.

Assessing the impact of services

Clearly, it is not 'normal' for parents to admit professionals into their family life. Before their child's disability was recognized, each family was just another family in the community. Thus, having to negotiate the service system is an unusual challenge (Begun 1996). Begun (1996: 49) identifies the tasks associated with this engagement:

> Few parents are prepared to serve 'executive parent' functions . . . that is, they have been socialized to care for their children, not to be recruiters, hirers and firers, advocates, consumers, coordinators, or professionals. Becoming a participant in the service delivery system is a unique developmental task for some parents, just as it is for the child with disabilities . . . It also may foster intimacies with people outside of the family that seem somewhat artificial.

When examining the potential effects of your work with families, it is clear that the quality of your relationship with family members – rather than the content of your service – will have the most impact on them. The quality of your service can be measured in many dimensions, the most crucial of which is parental satisfaction. This can be examined by asking the following questions, which are suggested by Bailey and colleagues (1998):

- Do the parents experience the service as making a positive difference to their child?
- Do the parents experience the service as making a positive difference to their family? This could be assessed by determining whether the service addresses their stated needs, is culturally and personally appropriate, and achieves their goals.
- Do the parents feel realistically optimistic about their child's future?
- Following intervention, are the parents confident that they can help their child to grow and learn?
- Do the parents find the service to be dependable: can they rely on its support in times of need? Programmes often cease when children reach a certain age and families are not followed up when a service has ended.
- Does the family have a positive view of professionals and the service system, making it more likely that they will consult professionals again if the need arises? The outcome of a lack of service continuity, for example, is that promises of support for the family are not fulfilled,

leading to parental disappointment and future reluctance to engage with other professionals for fear that the new service too will cease.
• Following intervention, does the family have a strong support system?

The second measure of the quality of your service is the extent to which the benefits of seeking and accepting professional support outweigh the costs. This equation has been termed the *response costs* of a service (Dunst et al. 1988). Although the family may experience some gains such as those listed above, securing and following up with the necessary services could create such turmoil in the family that members decide that the gains are just not worth it.

Another measure of parental satisfaction is the extent to which they are made to feel indebted to their service providers (Dunst et al. 1988). They are less likely to be satisfied if they are made to feel a sense of obligation or gratitude for a service which should be their right, not a privilege.

Indebtedness is less likely when the parent-professional relationship has a degree of reciprocity (Dunst et al. 1988). A reciprocal relationship will be restricted, as a true two-way friendship poses ethical issues (see Chapter 9), but parents can certainly contribute to professionals' knowledge and skills, and if professionals visit them at home, for instance, parents can offer hospitality and the common courtesies and expect these to be honoured by their visitors.

Parental satisfaction is less likely when we do not make clear to parents the aims of the programme; place them under pressure to participate in a service; emphasize the child's next step and thus do not give them time to appreciate the child's present level of functioning; emphasize the needs of the child with a disability over and above the needs of all the family; and impose too much structure on the child. Whereas individual practitioners might not be able to control some of the organizational limitations on their services which lead to parental dissatisfaction, these more practical difficulties arise 'at the coal face' of service delivery and so, with foresight, can in many cases be prevented as we now outline.

Ambiguous aims

The aims of intervention programmes are not always made clear to the parents. For example, parents often believe that early intervention activities will make their child 'catch up' by the school years. Information about the gains made from early intervention with environmental deprivation was popularized in the media at the time of the studies, with the result that some parents – and some professionals – believe that the gains made with environmentally deprived children are also possible for children with organic disabilities. Instead, we need to be clear with parents that, in most cases, our work with their children will not make the children 'normal' but it will prevent secondary difficulties – such as when a child's speech and language difficulties would cause later social problems.

Pressure to participate

The family may experience pressure to participate in educational programmes, especially if these are time-limited or if the child's age will soon make him or her ineligible for the service. Parents may also feel compelled to involve the child in a number of services at once, rather than in sequence. This places enormous pressure on them to accommodate all the necessary appointments.

Constant focus on the future

Most programmes assume that they have been successful when they have been able to hasten a child's developmental progress. However, this entrenches a deficit perspective of children and their families (Dunst 1985): the programme is always striving to have the child meet the next developmental milestone. This means that parents can be robbed of their child's present. When asked about their child's progress, unlike parents of children without disabilities, they do not respond with a story about something cute that their child did recently, but instead describe the next stage of development that they intend working on. Many is the time that I (Louise) have heard parents reply when asked how their child is doing: 'Really well. He's just mastered two-word utterances and we're beginning to work on three-words.' Reports such as this attest to the fact that their eye is always on the future, the next step. Present achievements are met with relief, rather than pleasure. While this can be a natural reaction to a child's difficulties, professional intervention can exacerbate it.

Lack of balance

At the same time as enhancing their confidence in their ability to meet their child's needs, parents need support to attend to their own needs and those of other family members; otherwise, their family can get out of balance in its exclusive focus on the child with disabilities.

Disadvantages of interventions for the child

Intervention programmes that are based on withdrawal of the child or on highly structured activities overseen by adults, can have many disadvantages for the child. These include: making the child reliant on and too compliant with adult direction; reducing the child's contact with peers; putting the child under pressure to achieve in all developmental domains at once – and instantly; and giving the child insufficient opportunities to consolidate and generalize skills.

These disadvantages imply that we cannot assume that more services will necessarily be of more help to families. Sometimes, they end up spending all their time making cups of tea for professional visitors and have little time left for meaningful family interaction or basic life tasks.

Summary

Families' service needs will change throughout the family life cycle and will depend on the match between available services and their present requirements. Professionals will need to listen to families' reports of their goals and, in collaboration with other workers and agencies, promote families' access to appropriate services and ensure that services are provided in a coordinated way.

Discussion questions

1. What are the needs that are most commonly felt by parents in your service or school? How adequately do services meet these needs? If there are shortcomings, to what do you attribute these?
2. In your work setting, are there any procedures in place for you to advocate for parents either within your service or school, or in outside settings?
3. Does your school or service provide any supports specifically to parents who themselves have disabilities? Does it offer anything for the children of parents with disabilities?

Chapter 7
Collaboration skills

They [the professionals] are very aware of the parents and for that child to be happy and comfortable, the parents have to be happy and comfortable as well. So they can approach it from the whole family perspective, not just from 'What can I do for this child?' but 'What can we do for this family?' . . . That's been really positive.

McKenzie (1993: 51)

Key points

- Parents and professionals approach each other with some, often unrealized, preconceptions. Awareness of these, and acceptance that their roles can complement each other's, will minimize conflict between them.
- Families function best when the parent/s are confident of their ability to lead their family. Professionals can ensure that they do not undermine this confidence by establishing truly collaborative partnerships that respect parents' goals and balance the needs of the child who has a disability with the needs of all the family.
- Professionals are often inadequately prepared in their initial training for such a collaborative relationship, not least because of the clinical model which underpins their work with children. When instead, they focus on children's and families' strengths, are aware of their own fallibility, take into account families' disparate cultural backgrounds, and are prepared to work in natural settings, they will be well equipped to meet families' needs.

Introduction

Having a child with special needs invariably engages parents with professionals and service agencies, and these relationships can continue throughout the child's life. This contact could commence at the child's birth or at a later time, depending on when the child's special needs are first noticed. It begins with a quest for an explanation for the child's apparent difficulties or lack of developmental progress, and continues when parents seek services to meet their child's identified needs.

In the past, professional intervention has typically centred on the child or the individual parent (usually the mother), mainly on teaching the mother skills for working with her child. However, today we realize that what is done for and with one family member affects all others. So, even when your work is mainly with a child, you must still consider what possible effect your service could have on the functioning of the whole family, on any individual members, and on the family members' relationships with each other. As we have described in previous chapters, expecting parents to carry out specialized programmes at home, for instance, may be considered best for the child but may interrupt the family's other functions which, if not carried out, can impact negatively on the child in other ways.

This is confirmed by my (Susan's) study (McKenzie 1993), in which parents of children with disabilities described professionals as helpful when they showed an understanding of both the child's and family's needs, provided information about the child's development and programme, assisted the child to develop skills and progress developmentally, and gave emotional support to families. One parent (McKenzie 1993: 39) described the value of the attention to her needs as well as those of her son:

> It was a great relief to know that there was some people out there that could actually help me, not just my son. They helped us a lot as a family I guess, the personal involvement. We are working together as a family – group team work together. It is fantastic.

Although many services lay claim to being 'family-oriented', they differ in terms of whether they are family-allied, family-focused or truly family-centred (Dunst et al. 1991). Only the last of these places the family in command of the services they receive and thus *family-centred* interventions are more likely to have positive influences on child, parent and family functioning (Dunst et al. 1991; Mahoney et al. 1990).

For families to remain in command of the services they receive, professionals need to exercise a range of skills. The first of these is to be aware of the image that you are projecting – that you present a personal rather than a professional facade – and that you do not impose on families preconceived notions of them or of disability; the second group of skills maintains parents' confidence in their ability to make decisions for their own family; and the third key set of skills is to be competent in the service that you provide their child. We will now examine each of these skill clusters in turn.

Managing perceptions

Sometimes, professionals are so keen to convey that they are professionally competent that they unwittingly create a barrier between themselves and the parents with whom they are working; for their part, parents can be overawed by or, conversely, sceptical about professionals and so they feel obliged to convey a 'good impression' to service providers. Such attempts at 'impression management' can get in the way of accurate and personal communication between parents and professionals (Berry and Hardman 1998; Mahoney et al. 1990; Seligman and Darling 1997). Key among these obstacles is the set of preconceptions that each party can have about the other.

Parents' perceptions of professionals

Before approaching your service or school, parents will have had previous contact with professionals, perhaps within but certainly outside of the disability field – for instance, when consulting their general medical practitioner. It may be that parents are more positively disposed to teachers than to other professionals, perhaps because teachers tend to have less status than, say, medical professionals. Conversely, parents may distrust teachers because of their own school experiences, because they feel that they have to compete with teachers for their children's loyalty and affection, or because their values do not coincide with those of the school or its teachers.

As well as generalized expectations, some parents have grown dissatisfied with professional services. This can come about for a number of reasons, many of which are beyond the control of individual professionals. First, professionals often represent organizations where financial restraints mean a loss of or reduction in services. Parents will feel the demise of services particularly keenly when they have fought to secure these particular services for their children. Second, even in good faith, professionals might have offered services that subsequently were not forthcoming or in some other way have left parents feeling let down.

Even without these unfortunate occurrences, parents usually enter into relationships with professionals when they are feeling most vulnerable. The common (but decreasing) attitude on the part of professionals that they 'know best' can leave parents feeling disrespected – and at a time when they are most sensitive to how they are treated.

Parents' vulnerability will perhaps be most acute during the early days of identifying and beginning to address their child's special needs.

Meanwhile, at this time professionals themselves might be feeling their way and might not yet be clear about the child's needs. In addition, they will not yet have built up an ongoing relationship with parents and so might not judge accurately how the parents wish to be related to. In their focus on the child, and with their own confusion and uncertainty, practitioners might forget to acknowledge the parents' own needs and skills. This may be viewed by the parents as lack of respect or regard for them and could result in negative perceptions of the professional.

In addition, many professionals work within large organizations or institutions, which can be constrained by their own procedures or 'red tape' that are not particularly responsive to the needs of consumers (Berry and Hardman 1998). By virtue of this, organizations may come to be seen as a hindrance rather than a help in parents' quest to meet their child's needs.

As a legacy of experiences with professionals which have been less than helpful, parents may either feel burnt out or might approach any new professional prepared to do battle. Thus, even before they meet you, parents' expectations of you may be tainted.

Professionals' view of disability

In the past, society has had a largely negative view of disability, and professional literature and research reflects this attitude. The result – particularly for professionals who did not specifically plan to work with children with disabilities – can be that they fear that they lack the necessary skills for dealing with these children. This is exacerbated when professionals expect too much of themselves, feel isolated, and feel that they lack the support and resources necessary to address these children's special needs (MacMullin and Napper 1993).

If professionals feel unprepared and under-resourced, they are likely to view disability negatively because they feel helpless. Their inability to 'cure' a child's disability can be discouraging, especially when they are accustomed to being competent and effective with a group of non-disabled children. It can help to remind themselves of the many skills they do have, and how these skills can be useful for all children, regardless of their abilities.

Negative perceptions are also occasioned by the fact that families consult professionals when they need something – usually information, but sometimes the support to enact that information. In other words, practitioners have most contact with parents in times of need. This may reinforce their negative view of the impact of a child's disability on families.

Professionals' view of families

As a result of their negative attitude toward disability, professionals often over-estimate the stressors that parents of children with a disability face and under-estimate the families' strengths and resources (Blackard and Barsch 1982), especially when the family comes from a different cultural background from themselves. This negative perception is not helped by the fact that some professional training courses and the disability litera-ture convey the view that any family with a disabled child is a 'disabled family' (Seligman and Darling 1997).

Faced with these inaccurate beliefs about the impact of the disability on the family and professionals' feelings of inadequacy, some practitioners can become despairing. Their hopelessness can then be communicated *indirectly* to the family, with the result that the family's self-esteem is lowered; and it can be reflected *directly* in their recommendations for the child, which can be based on their own attitudes rather than on the reality of the child's or family's needs and potential.

Thus, in order to establish successful relationships, professionals need to be aware of their attitudes towards parents and to disability. Turnbull and Turnbull (1997) list a range of professional attitudes that are unhelpful to parents and which get in the way of establishing a collabora-tive relationship with parents.

- Some professionals approach parents as if they were vulnerable or disabled themselves simply because they have a child with a disability. This attitude may exacerbate parents' feelings of powerlessness which might already have been triggered by the fact that they have needed to ask for professional assistance. It may leave them feeling patronized and resentful.
- Some professionals maintain 'professional distance' which is often experienced by families as a lack of empathy and an unwillingness to offer them support.
- Seeing the parent as the cause of the child's difficulties can feed into some parents' guilt on this issue.
- The view of parents as less observant, less perceptive, and less intelli-gent leads to discounting their views of their child and his or her needs, and will undermine a successful relationship with them.
- Adversarial or competitive relationships between parents and profes-sionals can arise as they share an interest in the child's welfare, while not necessarily sharing the opinion about how best to foster this. Acknowledging that they each want the best for the child is a useful place to start.

- Labelling parents as pushy, angry, 'in denial', resistant, or anxious is usually the result of inaccurate interpretation of parents' experience and motives, and is damaging to professionals' working relationship with parents. Labels not only criticize parents, but they also allow professionals to avoid taking responsibility for making the parent-professional relationship work.
- Furthermore, parents can feel resentful if it is assumed that they need to be taught specific skills for parenting their child (Foster et al. 1981).

Conclusion: managing perceptions

These preconceptions by both parents and professionals can make them especially keen to convey the 'right' impression to each other (Seligman and Darling 1997). However, these attempts at 'impression management' can sometimes be misinterpreted, such as when professionals visit the home and draw impressions of the parents on the basis of the state of the house. This is natural and probably unavoidable. However, in my (Louise's) experience, it seemed that parents could not win: if the house was spotless with not a toy in sight, the child's environment was seen to be 'deprived' and the mother 'obsessive'; but if the house was in the usual uproar that arises when young children are living in it, then the mother was characterized as 'disorganized'.

To avoid placing parents under pressure to project a certain image, you could convey that you intend to work alongside them, to carry out their wishes for their child – not to judge them or their family.

For their part, practitioners sometimes try to project a 'professional' image to families, which often views professionalism and emotions as incompatible (Summers et al. 1990). Yet, after their most immediate need for information that will help them to meet their child's needs, parents most want professionals to be sensitive – that is, to provide some emotional support (Summers et al. 1990). The apparently different needs of parents and professionals can be reconciled by being aware that, although professionals are not ordinarily parents' friends (because being paid to deliver a service is not friendship), professionals can still be *friendly*. That is, they can relate naturally as people, rather than adopting a formal 'professional' role.

Maintaining parental control

The second cluster of skills for collaborating with parents relates to ensuring that they maintain their confidence and ability to act as family leaders. All families have a natural hierarchy in which the parents' single or joint role is to oversee family functioning and be family leaders or decision makers (Foster et al. 1981). In other words, the parent or parents must be in executive control of the family, being the central figures around whom the family is organized, rather like the hub of a wheel. All family members are accorded equal rights to having their various needs met, but their roles within the family differ.

Professionals are only visitors in the family: they become part of a family's environment but are only a support or resource, rather than stake-holders or decision makers in the affairs of the family. Even when parents are stressed or burnt out and are encouraging you to take control for them, therefore, it is still crucial that you find ways to support the family without undermining the parents' confidence and sense of competence.

Adopt a collaborative, not an expert, stance

Even before any action is taken, the presence of a professional can undermine parents because they see themselves as needing help. Depending on the flavour with which that help is delivered, outside assistance can further undermine them, or strengthen their position as family leaders. An adviser who takes an expert stance may undermine the parents' confidence, giving them the impression that other people know how to work with their child, but they do not. In contrast, you will help parents to see themselves as just another family, with normal problems to solve, when you ask them what they want and need, devise together a realistic programme for their child, and involve them at each stage of your work with their child. Such actions will confirm to parents their status as family leaders, as the people who are able to solve their own problems.

It is also important that you do not impose on parents your own point of view, as this can undermine their ability to make their own decisions (Helm et al. 1998) and render them helpless or dependent.When this happens, the professional feels obliged to take on more and more decision making while the parents, in turn, feel more and more under-mined and so become increasingly passive. This can result in professional burnout or criticism of the family for not being sufficiently self-reliant when this passive role has been imposed on them rather than being their preference.

Respect parents

As a professional, you do not have to feel equally warmly towards everyone with whom you work, but you do have to act even-handedly to everyone. Respect involves accepting that others have reasons for their views - even if you do not entirely understand or you disagree with their perspective. It means recognising that parents have skills as parents and that you can learn from them about their child and their aspirations for him or her. Respect also requires you to avoid denigrating parents or their children with labels such as 'over-involved parents', or a 'stubborn' child - as criticism apportions blame and will detract from the quality of your relationship with parents.

Work on parental goals

Most of the literature in the field of family-professional partnerships says that professionals must focus on families' strengths and have faith in the ability of families to make choices and decisions that are in their own best interests. However, while this is a distinct improvement on focusing on parents' presumed inadequacies, the notion of assessing families' strengths still smacks of paternalism (Sokoly and Dokecki 1995) – or 'parentalism', if one wants to be gender-neutral. The concept still requires the professional to 'assess' the family, rather than simply explore with them what they need, in order to identify the services they require.

Instead respect involves listening to families' *needs* as parents report them, not assessing families' strengths – *or* deficiencies. It involves listening to the parents' perspective in order to appreciate the challenges they are facing. This, say Sokoly and Dokecki (1995: 191) gives the professional 'double vision' – that is, information from two perspectives – which will enrich the information on which decisions about services will be based.

Thus a clear element of maintaining parents' control of their family is assisting parents to achieve their own goals, not those defined for them by professionals. In this way, professionals do not have a stronghold on power but instead the parents steer the relationship with their service providers, directing it towards meeting the individual needs of all family members.

Balance individual and family needs

Another way in which professionals can safeguard parents' central role in their family is to ensure that we do not involve them too intensely in their child's programme. Although most of us who work with children with special needs regard the child as our highest – if not only – priority, in reality, a child suffers if his or her family is not coping. We might see an additional intervention for the child as beneficial, but the extra commitment could detract from the family's wellbeing and so the two potential consequences must be balanced against each other (see Chapter 9 also). While professionals will approach the task of assisting the child's development with great energy and enthusiasm, parents may not want – or be able

– to treat the child with the disability as the most important member of the family, even though the development of the child *is* very important to them. This point is expanded by Seligman (1979: 177):

> Some parents may genuinely want to be helpful and co-operative and have every intention of pursuing activities decided upon with the teacher, but somehow they find them impossible to initiate. For some parents, the demands of other members of the family and jobs may be so great that good intentions are difficult to implement. For others, engaging in mutually agreed upon activities with their child serves to highlight their child's deficiencies thereby increasing their anxiety.

While the roles of parents and professionals complement and supplement each other, their functions are not the same: professionals are paid to devote their attention to the welfare of the child who has a disability, while parents must address the needs of their entire family, both in the present and over the course of their child's life. Parents need to pace themselves for this long-term task: they are on a marathon rather than a 100-metre dash, and need time to relax and to meet everyone's needs (Turnbull and Turnbull 1986). This view is aptly expressed by a father (McKenzie 1996: 128):

> Our lives revolve around the children but we must also have a separate life too. If we have to learn to revolve around them, the children have to learn to revolve around Mum and Dad and the other child as well. You can't get totally bogged down and give 100% of your life to your child with a disability because if you do that you'll ignore his sister and you'll ignore yourselves. It's give and take.

You must balance the special needs of the child with the rights and needs of all family members and in light of each particular family's overall commitments. Otherwise, giving the needs of the child with the disability higher priority than the needs of other family members would make that child central to the family. In the short term during crises, this is natural, but if the exclusive focus on the child is maintained in the long term, it will undermine the parents' ability to lead the family (Frey 1984). The hierarchy is turned upside-down, with the child in control. This is unhealthy for overall family functioning, for children, and for parents' confidence.

Help parents to negotiate the service system

Another way that you can help parents to remain in command of the services they receive is to give them information about where they can find services and what to expect from these (Sussell et al. 1996). The ideal is that you will provide or ensure ongoing access to services for parents and their children, as their needs will change over time and because development does not cease in early childhood, which is when many services end. However, in reality there are often gaps in services and so it will be necessary at times to warn parents of these so that they can plan for them.

There will be times, as we noted in Chapter 6, when parents will also need help to negotiate services from other professionals or agencies. For instance, the use of abbreviations and acronyms, although just a minor issue in one way, can be very confusing and create a barrier to communication. Berry and Hardman (1998: 129) maintain that,

> Although parents can be expected to learn some common abbreviations, such as IEP for individualized education program, the use of initials for numerous programs, personnel categories, and agency names (which is common practice) is extremely confusing to parents and creates difference between professionals 'who know the code' and parents who feel they are being served 'alphabet soup'.

Sometimes, the terms used can even confuse members of other professions, in which case it can be helpful to seek clarification from members of other disciplines and to explain to parents those terms which they do not understand.

Limit your responsibilities

Parents need confidence that they can remain in control of their lives, even during crises. Obviously, it is important that you are responsive to a family's needs. However, if you make yourself endlessly available to parents or attempt to 'rescue' them in times of distress, you will unwittingly be telling them that you do not think that they can solve their own problems. In turn, they will become increasingly dependent on your support and advice. It may also delay their becoming uncomfortable enough to do anything about their problems: discomfort is a necessary stimulus for change.

Ensure that parents are not overwhelmed by services

Sometimes, parents appear not to be coping with their child's needs when, instead, they simply cannot manage the number of professionals who are involved with their family. In such cases, inadvertently, attempts to help have actually become the problem.

This was found to be so in a study which focused on quality of life for parents of children with disabilities (McKenzie 1996). One parent in that study said that she felt overwhelmed by the number of services offered.

She explained that coordinating the professionals with whom she was involved became a huge task in itself, even though her contact with some of these professionals consisted of only an occasional phone call. In response to her workload, the parent explained that she had become 'wiser' and reduced or 'streamlined' the number of professionals with whom she was involved.

Thus it may be that, at times, the solution to a family's or child's difficulties is simply to remove the multitude of professional helpers. Without complications from outside interference, the parents may be able to re-establish their own internal organization and take charge of themselves again (Madanes 1981).

Professional expertise

The third cluster of skills for working collaboratively with parents relates to delivering a competent service to families. This, however, does not imply that your expertise should place you in a superior position to families but that you are confident in your own skills and not defensive about sharing what you know with families or learning from them.

The first impediment to working in this collaborative fashion is when professionals work from what has been termed a 'clinical' model of service delivery which relies on professional diagnoses of problems (Seligman and Darling 1997).

Abandon a clinical approach

Professionals uniformly receive extensive training in their specialties; some child specialists will have trained with a particular focus on children; a comparatively rare few will be trained in disability; even fewer still are adequately prepared for providing family-centred services (Bailey et al. 1990a, 1990b, 1991). In fact, the very skills that make professionals competent in working with children with special needs can detract from their ability to work with these children's parents. This is because, in the main, professionals are trained in the clinical model of service delivery whereby their diagnosis is regarded as the only 'right' definition of a child's needs. And because only professionals can confer diagnoses, they are seen to be the experts while parents and children are less powerful at best and, at worst, are regarded as dysfunctional or 'sick'.

The clinical model of intervention has been described by Dunst (1985) as paternalistic, undermining and deficit-based. It ignores valuable information that parents could supply about their child's and family's goals, and overlooks the broader social and familial context in which the child's needs are experienced and dealt with. The clinical model implies that when parents are not 'coping', there is something wrong with them, rather than examining the possibility that the services are not meeting their needs (Seligman and Darling 1997). This possibility was verified by an early study which found that when appropriate services were provided to meet parents' needs, then their apparent 'emotional' difficulties abated (Schonell and Watts 1956).

Despite its medical-sounding title, the clinical approach is not confined to the health professions: education systems foster a similar use of labels and jargon whereby 'the problem' is often perceived as being located within 'the student' or 'the family'. Take, for example, behavioural difficulties, which are often seen to be a problem within the student or his or her family, when instead the actual trigger might be an inadequate teaching approach or unsuitable curriculum.

When people who have children with disabilities are forced to depend on and defer to the decisions of professionals, they are less able to exercise choice or have a sense of control over their own circumstances. These effects will directly detract from their quality of life (McKenzie 1996). As well, a lack of consideration for parents' views by professionals can lead to parents' ignoring professional advice which could otherwise be helpful, or withdrawing from services. This can take the form of 'shopping' for services – that is, parents simply 'vote with their feet'. They seek information elsewhere, thus creating additional work, anxiety and uncertainty (Helm et al. 1998).

Despite the obvious disadvantages of the clinical perspective, it persists – for a number of reasons (Seligman and Darling 1997). In the first place, most practitioners are trained exclusively in the clinical model and so they are not well prepared professionally to adopt an alternative way of operating. Furthermore, because most professionals employ the model, they can communicate more easily with each other, as they share the same perspective and language with its reliance on diagnoses, labels and jargon.

The clinical approach also reduces uncertainty for professionals. When apparent 'problems' can be labelled and clustered, this suggests which intervention is appropriate. Children's progress can be measured quantitatively and remediation can involve changing the child or family to meet professionally defined goals (Seligman and Darling 1997). If, instead, professionals were to consider all aspects of family functioning rather than just the 'deficits' of the child with special needs, intervention would be more complex.

In place of the clinical approach, professionals will have to relinquish their dominant role by considering family needs and acknowledging the strengths and skills of parents (Seligman and Darling 1997). This means becoming less possessive about their own professional knowledge, and being willing to engage in a two-way exchange of information with parents. It takes some well-attuned communication skills (see Chapter 8) and a good deal of confidence about their own area of specialty to feel safe enough to abandon a dominant stance.

Respect the child

The most powerful way to build rapport with parents is a professional's success with their child. However, the clinical perspective's reliance on diagnosis highlights children's 'deficiencies', particularly in the assessment process. Instead, assessment needs to focus on children's strengths as well as their needs, so that prejudice and notions of difference do not dominate children's future (Branson et al. 1988; Cook et al. 1996; Deiner 1998).

On the other hand, it is important to acknowledge that a label or diagnosis can be very helpful to parents if they have undergone a long period of concern about the reason for their children's difficulties or lack of developmental progress. Assessment and labelling can also serve a social justice function by allocating resources to the most needy. Given the potential benefits of labels, but the opposing costs to children and their families, conferring a diagnosis needs to be handled with sensitivity and respect. (Some suggestions for communicating diagnoses to parents are given in Chapter 8.)

Once an intervention is under way, success will require you to teach the child functional skills, rather than simply the next step in a developmental sequence without regard for its usefulness to the child and family; to ensure that the child can take an active part in his or her own learning; to identify how the child communicates and assist parents to recognize their child's cues when these are atypical; and to use whatever valid instructional strategies will promote the child's development (Hanson 1987).

Professional fallibility

Although it is acknowledged that professionals have specialised knowledge, we also need to recognise that we can and do make mistakes in our work. When mistakes occur, acknowledging them is the best chance we have of mending our relationship with family members.

It is worth remembering that because of their frequent contact with professionals, parents of children with disabilities are more likely than other groups to encounter professional errors and failure (Seligman and Darling 1997), not just because professionals are human and inevitably make mistakes but also because medical and educational knowledge about disability is not complete.

Nevertheless, at the time of the discovery of a child's disability, parents are likely to rely on the expertise of professionals. (Only later do they challenge that authority if their trust is betrayed.) Parents are often having to hear difficult news at a time when they are extremely vulnerable and very sensitive to how that information is conveyed to them. The result is that in the early days of determining a child's special need, parents' expectations for professionals can be unrealistically high, making disillusionment almost inevitable.

McKenzie (1993) conducted a study which focused on the perceptions of professionals by parents of young children with disabilities. Some parents reported that medical staff provided a diagnosis prior to gathering sufficient information. In a few cases, these specialists had painted a bleak picture of the child's future, which had caused unnecessary distress to the family. The following is a quote from one father (McKenzie 1993: 54):

> . . . the doctor had hardly examined him, read a piece of paper and then watched him crawl across the floor and said, 'He'll never walk.' That was a real tail kick for my wife and I. At that stage our child was probably too young to understand, but it didn't do anything for our morale. Now at four, he's walking. He walks!

The message here is that you are most likely to be of assistance to families if you are aware of the limits and boundaries of your own knowledge and expertise, and if you remain sensitive and honest in your interactions with parents.

Cultural awareness

A collaborative relationship with all parents is possible only when we are aware of cultural differences and our own cultural biases. It is incumbent on professionals to ensure equal access to and participation in services by all families (Harry et al. 1995, in Sexton et al. 1997). Service provision across cultures involves two important principles (Roberts et al. 1998): first, professionals and services ought to respect and honour diverse belief systems and not expose families to services that are racist or 'culturally destructive', second, while bigotry assumes that differences between people make them unequal, 'colour blindness' assumes that the differences do not matter (Stonehouse 1991b). Rather than having either preconception, we must recognize that members of non-majority cultures are often disadvantaged in relation to their health, education and social conditions, and that ignoring their racial, cultural or religious experiences would dismiss a vital part of their identity (Gonzalez-Mena 1997).

Sometimes cultural differences between families and professionals can lead to misunderstandings, especially if we stereotype families and their view of disability on the basis of their ethnicity or social background. On this point, Seligman and Darling (1997) stress that within most groups in the community, there is considerable variation in beliefs and practices and so professionals cannot assume anything about individuals on the basis of their affiliation with a culture or religion.

Foley (1975, in Seligman and Darling 1997) and others have listed some recommendations for professionals who work with disadvantaged African Americans, which could equally well apply to disadvantaged cultural groups elsewhere:

• Earn the family's confidence by providing practical assistance, such as access to better housing, financial support, or support services such as respite care.
• Be aware of differences in communication styles, including indirect and incomplete messages.
• Ensure that you do not compound the helplessness of such families by your intervention.
• Include extended family members when the nuclear family regards them as part of their unit.
• Ask about their beliefs concerning their needs and cultural practices (e.g. child discipline), and do not violate these with your suggestions for the child's programme.
• It can be very beneficial when professionals speak the parents' native language; interpreters are a useful alternative.
• Professionals must be able to accept a range of culturally and socially diverse philosophies. Parents' self-esteem must be confirmed.
• Schedule appointments flexibly to account for parents' transport difficulties or work shifts. For example, call factory workers in their breaks only, so that they do not incur their employers' wrath at their receipt of personal calls during work time.

Seligman and Darling (1997) conclude that before we can begin to meet the needs of families from cultures other than our own, we need to understand how they perceive their needs within their personal and cultural context.

Use a natural environment

Collaboration will be enhanced or compromised according to the setting in which you deliver your service. Some settings can be unfamiliar or even threatening to parents. Schools, hospitals or clinics are the home turf of professionals and so it is easy for them to assume control in these settings (Berry and Hardman 1998; Seligman and Darling 1997). The bureaucratic atmosphere in large facilities can also undermine parents and depersonalize them, so that they feel they are just another case number within an impersonal system.

Clinic appointments can set up unrealistic expectations for those carrying on the programme later in more natural settings such as the home or school. For example, a speech pathologist who teaches a child in a clinic can ensure that distractions are minimized, whereas a parent at home cannot stop a younger sibling from interrupting the child. The parent might feel discouraged that she cannot work as successfully with the child as the speech pathologist can and so might discontinue the programme.

Home based services can show parents how to conduct a programme amongst these normal distractions, they have the advantage of avoiding transport difficulties, and can help parents and children feel more at ease. But, on the other hand, the perceived need to create a good impression can also cause parents to feel uncomfortable with home visits. Therefore, before undertaking a programme, it can pay to offer the parent a choice of venue if possible.

Summary

When working with families, professionals need to allow parents to decide on a role for themselves that meets their needs. We must realize that their needs will change over time, leading to fluctuating levels of involvement in their child's programme.

Above all, it is crucial to ensure that parents maintain their confidence in their own skills for meeting their child's needs and retain their ability to act as leaders in their family. Therefore, you will need to:

- Consider the impact of your work on the whole family.
- Remember that professionals are usually only small stakeholders in a child's life compared with his or her parents. Be a resource and source of support to families, not a decision-maker or family leader.
- Resist professional dominance; allow families to see that you trust their judgement, and stand by their decisions. Maintain a healthy family hierarchy by providing support, information and practical assistance to families.
- Make sure that each of you understands what the other expects from you.
- Being 'helpful' to the parents may make matters worse for them by undermining their confidence in their ability to make decisions for themselves. Therefore, provide only those services they ask for, and do not over-burden them with help.
- Avoid judging and labelling parents. Try to remain sensitive and understanding even if you find it difficult to understand a family's values or

choices. You can understand *that* they feel as they do, even if you do not understand *why*.

Despite the many barriers to empowering relationships between parents of children who have disabilities and their professional service providers, both share a common bond: they both want what is best for the child. They may have differing opinions about what would be 'best' or how to attain that 'best', but, ultimately, goodwill and skilled communication will go a long way towards establishing relationships in which the skills of both the parents and the professionals can inform each other, enrich their relationship, and promote better outcomes for the child with the disability and his or her family.

Discussion questions

1. Given your professional role, how can you best take account of families' needs at the same time as working with a child with special needs?
2. What sort of impression of yourself and your role do you try to convey to parents? Having read this chapter, do you want to make any changes to how you approach them?
3. How can your own professional expertise become one of the resources that can support parents?

Chapter 8
Communicating with families

The professional as 'scientist' knows how to teach, carry out therapy, and has other specialized knowledge about working with children with disabilities. The professional as 'relationship builder' knows how to interact on a personal level, has the ability to listen to concerns and issues, does not stereotype, does not compare and sees the child in a broader system than just the educational setting.

Bennett et al. (1998: 119)

Key points

- Collaboration between families and professionals depends on effective communication.
- Effective communication comprises sets of skills which can be learned and practised. However skilled we may be, we can all improve these communication skills.
- The aspects of communication addressed in this chapter include active listening, assertion, exchanging information with families and managing conflict and solving problems.

Introduction

Successful collaboration relies on many factors among which are knowledge about families and skilled communication with them. To contribute to knowledge about families who have members with disabilities we have provided information about their circumstances and the challenges they may encounter. Further, we have maintained that each family is unique and that you will need to consult with family members to determine their goals and priorities to guide your work with them.

The need to develop collaborative relationships with families will always accompany change to the teaching role; where students have special needs or disabilities, there are often increased demands for collaboration with parents. In addition, collaboration with staff within your own environment and with professionals from organizations outside your own is often part of working with students who have disabilities.

Interpersonal skills

Successful communication is made up of generic sets of interpersonal skills which can be learned and honed. These skills constitute the fundamentals for collaborating with family members and other professionals with whom we are involved. Each set of skills has a place in the communication process and many of us will feel more competent in using some compared with others. In this chapter, the skills of listening, being assertive, and resolving problems are discussed in relation to working with families who have members with disabilities. They are then applied to situations where you must exchange information with parents or handle parents' complaints.

Most texts on communication skills mention the need to build rapport with others. In our experience, rapport is not content-free and not necessarily built by exchanging pleasantries about the weather. Although social chat can be useful, true rapport will develop only when parents experience you as listening to what they have to say. Second, they need to know that you are competent at providing the service that they require for their child. Third, rapport will be cemented when not only what you do is appropriate for their needs, but how you work with them respects and validates them.

Listening

It is probably true that all of us could be better at listening. It is a skill that we can always improve upon. It is integral to collaboration with families because:

- Listening to others sends messages to them about their worth. Listening to parents sends a direct message that their views are worth hearing.
- Listening to parents fosters collaborative relationships and shows them that the model from which you are operating is not one of professional dominance.
- Open communication releases tension and nurtures a relationship. You can provide support to family members by listening to them. 'Just talking' to someone who will 'just listen' can often reduce the burden of worries or stresses.

- People do not always clearly understand what is happening in their own situations. When they can speak to someone who will really listen, they can organize their thoughts. For some parents, clarity may be the first step to managing their circumstances.
- Parents are sometimes unclear about educational options or other issues concerning their children. Allowing parents to discuss their options openly helps them to understand these. Reflecting content back to parents can assist them because they can hear themselves think.

'Real' listening requires courage, generosity and patience on our part (Mackay 1994). It requires courage, because if we seriously entertain another's ideas it makes us vulnerable as we move out of our own comfort zone and see another point of view that could challenge our own or reveal it as flawed. Listening requires our generosity, because it is something we do for another person even when the message is less than welcome or is unattractive to us. Finally, listening requires patience because we need to suspend our own thoughts, questions and judgements and make sure we have understood the message before responding to it.

It is not easy to remain patient when listening – as evidenced in everyday interpersonal interactions when we interrupt with questions or our own thoughts before we have understood another's message. Mackay (1994: 149) claims that, 'If words were actions, we would never tolerate the interpersonal violence which we inflict on each other in the name of conversation (or, worse, in the name of communication)'. This perhaps makes it painfully clear that listening is not easy, yet it also suggests that if we understand listening as a skill that doesn't come easily to most of us, it is also one which we can improve with practice.

Specifically, 'active listening' involves giving other people attention, being willing to listen rather than trying to impose your own ideas on them, noticing their feelings as well as their words, and actively reflecting what they are saying by providing non-verbal and verbal feedback to show them that you have heard what they have said.

Attention

When you give someone your attention, you are taking the first step in active listening. It indicates that you are ready and willing to listen to what another person has to communicate. Your body language can indicate this when you give a speaker eye contact and face toward him or her in an open posture.

Attentive silence

Attentive silence and attentive body posture are non-verbal messages that convey that you are ready to listen. This is summed up by Robert Benchley (in Bolton 1987: 48) who said: 'Drawing on my fine command of language, I said nothing'.

Questions are not always helpful in the process of listening because they can be interpreted as interruptions or diversions. As a general rule, questions do not usually make a great contribution to the process of listening as they can make speakers feel that they are being subjected to an inquisition. However, when carefully constructed, a few questions may help speakers to clarify their thoughts.

Minimal encouragers

In attending to another, the listener can use 'minimal encouragers' to indicate that he or she is listening to what is being said. Minimal encouragers include such utterances as 'mm-hmm' or 'uh-huh' which are usually accompanied by nodding. It is important to note however that it is the delivery and execution of these minimal encouragers that determines their effectiveness. One type of delivery and execution will denote sincerity while another will denote 'mock listening' which consists of 'nodding, smiling, making little noises of assent or encouragement – while we are actually working on the much more interesting task of deciding what we are going to say next' (Mackay 1994: 143).

Door openers

Door openers are invitations to communicate. They are especially useful if you sense that someone wants to talk but needs encouragement. Door openers typically have four elements (Bolton 1987: 41):

1. A description of the other person's body language: 'There's a spring in your step today'.
2. An invitation to talk or continue talking: 'Want to talk it over?'
3. Silence – allowing the person space in which to respond or at least decide whether or not he or she wants to take up your offer to talk.
4. Attention – giving the person eye contact and displaying a posture of involvement.

Bolton (1987) reminds us that not all four elements will always be present in a door opener and that a number of factors, including the relationship between individuals and their respective roles, will determine the most effective door opener in a particular situation.

Reflective listening

When you hear another's message, try to tease out the feeling behind the message. This can be difficult when their feelings are strong, as even the positive emotions such as joy or excitement can unsettle us – and it can be especially difficult to accept when someone is angry. When you have listened for feelings, it can be helpful to reflect these back. You can reflect the content, the feeling, or the meaning behind what the person is telling you. You can do this by paraphrasing or summarizing what she or he is saying. Bolton (1987: 51) describes paraphrasing as giving:

- a concise response;
- stating the essence;
- of the content;
- in the listener's own words.

Let's say that a parent has been telling you that his child is being bullied by others in her class. Depending on the actual words which the parent has used, you might respond with something like, 'So you're upset that she is being teased by the other children and you would like me to speak to them to get it to stop.'

At first, reflecting back what someone is saying can seem very false – silly, almost. It sounds as if you will be saying the obvious. Or you might worry about getting it wrong. But remember that a parent may be dealing with a range of emotions at once which she or he may not be understanding completely, in which case your comments and reflection can help clarify these.

In conclusion to the discussion of active listening it is important to point out that it is a specialized skill common to most counselling techniques. It does encourage people to speak openly, and so strong feelings can emerge. Therefore while active listening is a valuable tool that you can employ, you also need to operate within the realm of your training and refer family members to other agencies or professionals if problems emerge that are outside your expertise.

Roadblocks to communication

Now that we have examined the skills involved in listening, it is useful to consider what listening is *not* – that is, to identify some common conversation habits that, rather than encouraging conversation, instead discourage other people from talking to us. Gordon (1970) described twelve such habits and termed them 'roadblocks to communication'. These are divided into the categories of judging, sending solutions, and avoiding the other person's feelings.

Judging

It is important that you accept people's feelings, even when they are different from your own. This means not judging someone for feeling a certain way. For example, a parent may react to her child's poor exam result in a manner that seems to you to be an over-reaction. The strong feelings expressed by the parent may seem far too intense for the situation.

The following list of roadblocks includes examples of responses to the parent's feelings.

* *Criticizing* or *blaming* may involve comments such as: 'Don't you think you're expecting too much of him?' or 'Perhaps he could do better if you didn't put so much pressure on him'.
* *Praising*, in an effort to talk the parent out of her feelings: 'You have worked so hard to help him with his work that I'm sure he will do better on the next test'.
* *Name-calling* is similar to criticising or blaming and may take such a form as this: 'Don't you think you are being overanxious?' It usually involves assigning some sort of label and can be a recurrent feature of staffroom conversation: 'She's over-involved'.
* *Diagnosing* or *interpreting* may be an attempt to tell the parent what her 'real' problem is and it will often involve 'fishing' or probing for information to prove that your interpretation is correct: 'Perhaps you are so upset because you still really haven't accepted that he has a disability' or 'You're feeling so upset because you think that she will not develop without this programme?'

Sending solutions

Sometimes, instead of listening, we are quick to tell others what we think they should do. Sending our own solutions can take five forms.

* *Directing* the person to stop what he or she is feeling: 'It's not necessary for you to be so worried about this', or more commandingly, 'Don't worry about it.'
* *Threatening* imposes your solution on the person and is often presented as an ultimatum: 'If you can't find time to help him at home, he won't learn.'

- *Preaching* explains why someone should feel differently: 'You should not let this get you down, it's not that bad'.
- *Interrogating* involves questioning to get to the bottom of the problem: 'How difficult has this been for you?' or 'Just what has upset you so much about this?' This type of probing suggests that you can find a solution for the person instead of trusting him or her to find one.
- *Advising* is an attempt to impose a positive solution: 'Perhaps you could spend more time with him at home' or 'I think it would help if you took some pressure off her.'

Because we want to help others, giving advice is probably the most common of the roadblocks that any of us use. However, giving advice has many disadvantages. It usually dismisses a person's concerns as 'easily solvable' and therefore quite trivial. By giving advice you can send a message that you do not think that others are capable of finding solutions for themselves. When people act on your advice they may see themselves as unable to solve their own problems which may make them dependent on you, and it may damage your relationship with them because they feel patronized. Further, if people act on your advice and things turn out badly, it is easy for them to lay the blame on you. On the other hand, if they do not follow your advice, they may feel guilty.

Often when people say, 'I want your advice', it is code for 'I want to talk something over with you', or perhaps more pertinently, 'I want you to listen to what I have to say'. It is also important to distinguish between 'giving advice' and 'providing information'. The latter involves laying out the facts and discussing the possible outcomes of different courses of action based on your experience and expertise, whereas the former is characterized by directing or influencing people to take a particular course of action.

Avoiding the other person's feelings

A third group of roadblocks tries to take the heat out of others' feelings, usually because their emotions disturb us. This class of roadblocks includes:

- *Distracting* the person from the issue at hand. This includes introducing an alternative subject: 'It is terrific, though, that she has become so popular with the other students,' when you were discussing something else altogether which was worrying the parent.
- *Logical argument*, which sends the message: Don't feel – think. It may take a form like this: 'Being teased by the others is all part of the

learning process, he can't expect to get along with everybody all the time.'

- *Reassuring* tries to change how the person is feeling and sends a message that you are uncomfortable with the expression of feelings: 'Don't let this upset you. It's a small setback in the larger scheme of things.' Reassurance tends to discount the person's feelings and is dismissive in the sense that it sends a message that you do not want others to reveal their feelings.

The thirteenth roadblock

A thirteenth communication roadblock has been added to the 'dirty dozen' by Bolton (1987), who suggests that accusing other people (blaming them), or feeling guilty ourselves, for using the communication roadblocks is in itself a communication stopper.

If you have had an attack of guilt while reading about the roadblocks, take heart. It is never too late to hone your listening skills. One way to start is to notice the roadblock that you use most, and work on stopping that. Then work on your others in turn. And remember to be kind to yourself and to notice when you have genuinely listened at a time when in the past you would have used a roadblock.

Another useful exercise is to take a blank sheet of paper and divide it vertically down the middle. On the left-hand side, write down one change in your life that you have been wanting to make for a while, but have not been able to begin. It could be that you want to exercise more, eat less of particular foods, or make some other kind of change – whatever. On the right-hand side of your sheet of paper, write what you have been saying to yourself about failing to make the changes. Our bet is that you'll find that you use the roadblocks on yourself and have tended to criticize or preach at yourself about your failure. The roadblock that you use on yourself is probably the same one that you use with others. Now that you are aware of this, you can practise more genuine listening – both to your own needs and to those of others.

Assertion

A second category of communication skills is assertion. It enables us to express our thoughts, needs and feelings in an open and honest manner that does not violate the rights of others. It begins with the word 'I' to tell others about how you are responding to their actions. This distinguishes assertiveness from aggression, which uses the word 'you' to tell other people about themselves.

The most commonly recognized form of an assertive message is the one that follows the formula:

'When you (do x)
I feel (whatever)
because (it affects me in this way).'

However, some people find this too confronting – either to deliver or receive! An alternative which you may find most helpful in your interactions with parents and other professionals, is 'empathic assertion' (Jakubowski and Lange 1978). This type of assertive message begins with a statement which conveys that you understand the other person's point of view; next, it states your position; and, third, it asks what you should both do. For instance:

'I understand that you want your son to walk to the local shop to buy his lunch. However, it is my duty to ensure that students remain on the school grounds at all times during school hours. So what could we do so that he can have some lunch while staying at school?'

'It's clear that you want your daughter to spend more class time on handwriting, yet I have to consider the needs of the other children and balance the time they each spend on the various curricular areas. How can we get around that?'

Empathic assertion does not 'put down' other people; rather it acknowledges them and their view while clearly stating your own position. In the examples above, it opens the possibilities for negotiation: your assertive message does not have to be the last word on an issue. However, the real value of empathic assertion comes from the fact that it demonstrates to others that we are willing to listen to them and that we acknowledge that they feel justified in their concerns.

Another advantage of empathic assertion is that it tends not to provoke the defensive reaction that more confronting forms of assertion can. People who have received an assertive message can sometimes become upset, angry, defensive, tearful, or embarrassed. In that case, it is clear that you need to revert to listening skills and reflect their feeling. This defensiveness, however, is sometimes avoided by the empathic form of assertion.

Resolving conflict and solving problems

A third cluster of communication skills is useful for solving problems and disputes. Even though we may work hard at communicating effectively, disputes are inevitable when people work together. There will always be times when what one person believes is at odds with what someone else wants. Although most of us see this as a negative feature of life, resolving such conflicts can teach us about our own needs and values, and gives us the chance to learn more about other people's.

When attempting to solve a particular problem, your aim will be to find a solution that is acceptable to everyone concerned. This can be achieved through collaborative problem solving which involves six steps.

1. The people concerned agree to talk it over – the parties must be willing to work together to reach a solution.
2. Each person listens to the other's point of view and then expresses what he or she wants assertively – but not aggressively. This should result in a clear picture of each person's perspective and what each person wants. Even if the parties do not agree at this stage they should at least have reached a level of understanding. At this point many conflicts dissolve as people find they misunderstood each other and that they do share common ground. In other words, completion of these first two steps often takes the heat out of a dispute.
3. Together, you come up with ideas of what you *could* do so that both of you might be able to meet your needs. At this stage you do not evaluate how practical the suggestions are, just brainstorm all possibilities.
4. Next, decide which of the options you *will* act on. You may want to use a process of elimination to work through the suggestions but do not choose a compromise that pleases no one; instead, work on a solution that meets both needs to some degree.
5. Decide when and how to carry out your solution and act upon it.
6. Finally, once it is in place, check whether the solution is working.

Negotiating a solution with which all parties agree means that they are likely to be motivated to carry out the decision because they participated in making it and it is not imposed on them by someone else. Therefore, you do not have to enforce the solution and you can both work with – not struggle against – each other.

Listening to the other person – be it a parent or a colleague – means that you do not have to guess what he or she needs and you do not have to come up with a solution by yourself. This means that you have more chance of finding a high-quality solution, because two heads are always better than one, and it reduces your workload by having someone else with whom to share the decision-making.

Applying these skills in practice

There are many occasions when you will need to exercise these three clusters of communication skills in your relationships with parents. At times you will be wanting to pass on information to them about their son's or daughter's progress, telling them of your concerns about their child, solving problems, or handling complaints.

One of the best ways to avoid misunderstandings and conflict is to keep the lines of communication open. For instance, parents will probably be more amenable to your raising of a concern about their child's behaviour if the occasion represents one of many communications they have had with you. I (Susan) once found members of a staff team were surprised when a parent responded defensively to their raising concerns about her child's behaviour; yet, from the mother's perspective, during the months preceding this she had heard little from the staff except that her son was 'doing fine', and she was understandably confused when she suddenly found her son described as 'regularly hurting others'.

Keeping the lines of communication open also ensures that we build a relationship with family members. This means that when the content of communications is sensitive or difficult, the relationship is strong enough to support successful communication.

Some families may prefer that information is provided in written format, while others with reading difficulties would prefer a verbal exchange of information. Many students with disabilities will have a communication book which travels with them in which teachers can communicate with parents to keep them informed about their child's activities. Teachers can also provide parents with readings or resources to read in their own time and follow up by checking that the information was appropriate and whether they require further information. In addition the telephone, e-mail and the internet are useful means of communication now that many schools have their own web sites.

Exchanging information regarding student progress

Most parents are keen to hear how their children are progressing at school. School reports or samples of work and student profiles are a formal means of providing such information. Just as important are the incidental or informal opportunities to share something with parents about their child's progress. For parents of children with disabilities, ongoing concern about their child's development or progress at school can be a source of worry or tension. This means that they will be particularly keen to hear about positive aspects of their child's behaviour at school as they may often receive predominantly negative information about their child. They will also want to hear about their child's friendships, enjoyment of particular activities or progress in non-academic subjects. Giving feedback about the whole range of the child's development or experiences at school can provide some relief for parents from the focus on academic progress.

Sometimes a phone call from school can mean only one thing: there is a problem. To avoid contact between parents and schools or other service providers occurring only when there are problems, proactive contacts such as those we have just described can be established through informal communications at pick-up and delivery times; coffee mornings; notes home about a child's progress; newsletter items about individuals' and the whole class's current projects – and so on.

Delivering sensitive information

Sometimes teachers are the first to have concerns about a child's development or progress. On such occasions, you will need to convey your concerns to the child's parents. When conveying potentially upsetting information about children to their parents, Ginott (1972: 277–8) cautions:

> When a teacher talks to parents about their children, he [or she] inevitably intrudes on family dreams . . . What the teacher says about the child touches on deep feelings and hidden fantasies. A concerned teacher is aware of the impact of his [or her] words. He [or she] consciously avoids comments that may casually kill dreams.

This means that you will need to plan your meeting very carefully, in order that the parents will feel comfortable and that there is enough time to discuss your concerns and to listen to their reactions (Abbott and Gold 1991). On such occasions, it is not appropriate to pre-empt a diagnosis or make a judgement that you are not trained or qualified to make – for example by saying something such as, 'I believe Sam may have attention deficit disorder.' Without offering a diagnosis, it is appropriate, however, to raise concerns with the parent and perhaps to recommend some kind of assessment: 'Sam is having some difficulties concentrating here at school. Have you noticed this at home?'

Sometimes, we anticipate that the parents will be shocked at our questions and, indeed, some may be surprised because they had not noticed that their child was having difficulties. Often, however, they are well aware of the child's problems and are grateful that you are interested enough to raise your concerns with them. Sometimes, the act of doing so gives them some relief as they have been worried for some time.

Usually parents are aware of their children's behaviour and are able to offer useful information that can help you in responding to it. They may tell you that there have been major changes at home or some family crisis that has affected the child's behaviour at school, which could help you identify how best to respond to the new behaviour.

Once a child has been identified as having some type of disability or learning difficulty it is important that you do not predict the child's future progress or levels of achievement. As children and families are individual, a particular type of disability does not necessarily indicate what the child may or may not be able to achieve in future.

Suggestions for discussing diagnoses

Parents need professionals to be honest and specific in their diagnosis of the child's difficulties, while also making clear whether a label is descriptive, explanatory or prognostic (see Chapter 6). It is important that professionals do not delay imparting negative information out of some misguided desire to shield the parents. This is usually self-protective, while severely harming the parents. Turnbull and Turnbull (1990: 110) provide a list of suggestions for explaining a child's diagnosis to the family:

- Convey the information in terms that avoid mystification and jargon. Explain any specialized terms that must be used.
- Provide full and honest communication about the condition of the child.
- Repeat the information in many different ways and at many different times.
- Try to tell both parents at the same time if at all possible.
- Encourage parents to ask questions.
- Discuss the limits of professional knowledge about the child's present condition and ultimate development.
- Present a balanced perspective – discuss possible positive outcomes as well as limitations.
- Avoid a patronizing or condescending attitude.
- Encourage parents to join a support group or introduce them to a family who is coping successfully with a son or daughter who has a similar exceptionality. (However, timing is crucial here, as exposing parents too soon to all the realities of their child's condition can be too confronting for them - see Chapter 6).
- Realize that the parents will need time to consider the diagnosis: set up another conference.
- Allow parents time to express their feelings and accept those, even if you do not understand them fully.
- If parents respond with anger, avoid being defensive: their attack is on the diagnosis, not you. Continue to be supportive and accepting.
- Discuss what the parents can say when they tell brothers and sisters and other family members about their child's special needs.
- Suggest reading materials and other resources without, however, overwhelming parents too soon with too much information. Let them guide you about what information they need and when.

- Assure families that you will be available as a resource to them in the future (as long as this is likely to be true).

Simpson (1990: 44) offers this conclusion about conveying diagnoses:

> Specifically, professionals must accurately and compassionately communicate diagnostic findings and recommendations, help families secure appropriate services and support families through what is an extremely difficult time. As suggested, initial positive and supportive interactions between parents and families establish a basis for future effective communication and an overall effective parent-professional partnership.

It will help two-parent families if you can speak with both parents about your concerns. If this cannot be arranged, then you could tape your conversation so that the parent who could not attend can at least listen to the taped conversation. You will need to pass on the invitation for that parent to contact you with any questions that arise from hearing the tape. Taping the conversation can also provide repetition by letting parents replay the tape as often as they need to. It will avoid the problem that parents who have received a shock sometimes tune out vital details about their child's needs and plans for meeting them.

Before the meeting, ensure that you have updated your knowledge of which agencies are available to provide the type of assessment the child requires. This information will include waiting time, costs and contact phone numbers. The more specific your information can be, the easier it will be for the parents to follow up your concerns promptly.

Sometimes, when you draw parents' attention to their child's difficulties or recommend a particular intervention, parents will ask for a second opinion. Their search for a second opinion may arise from legitimate dissatisfaction with services, a desire to have as much information as possible, or a wish to work with professionals who share their perspective (Turnbull and Turnbull 1990). In such cases, it is easy to become defensive. But keep in mind that most professional opinion has only a tenuous basis in fact and instead comes through a profession's particular way of viewing the world. Most professional conclusions are conjecture and are open to doubt: we seldom actually *know* for certain whether a child will or will not develop particular skills into the future. All that you can do is convey to the parents what your experience of similar children has taught you, and they can make the judgement about whether that is likely to apply to their child.

Remember that your goal is not to prove yourself, but to obtain appropriate services for the child. Therefore, when parents do seek a second opinion, Turnbull and Turnbull (1990) suggest that you accept and respect their right to disagree with you. It can help to check back in your mind whether you may have used ambiguous terms which the parents need to clarify. It might be useful to compare what assessment information you presently have about the child and identify the gaps that the parents feel remain. If this leaves questions unanswered, then you should encourage them to consult another practitioner.

Problem solving with parents

When individual students are experiencing a difficulty at school, it is wise to avoid giving advice to their parents (Coleman 1991) but rather to collaborate with them to find a solution. You might use the collaborative problem-solving steps which were outlined earlier in this chapter. However, at times, parents might suggest a solution that is impractical or unethical. If you argue against their suggestion, you might undermine them; but neither can you enact their solution. In this case, Heath (1994) suggests that, before selecting which course of action you will follow, together you and the parents could:

- identify the types of solutions which are possible in the circumstances;
- restate your goals for the student;
- identify the relevant characteristics of the student – temperament, age, size (as this affects the child's ability to dominate his or her peers, for instance), interests, responses to earlier disciplinary attempts, and so on;
- identify the needs of the people involved;
- identify the feelings of those who are involved.

Handling complaints

Your first task when parents come to you with a complaint will be to listen. You will need to reflect what they are saying and acknowledge their feelings. When they are expressing these offensively, however, you might have to add an assertive statement such as, 'I accept that you are angry that Simon's jacket has gone missing, although I do not like how you are saying it'. The next step is to state that you have a common interest – namely, providing the best possible care for their child. You might add in what way your meeting is intended to advance that purpose – for example: 'I wonder how we could ensure that his clothes do not get lost again?'

There will be occasions when the behaviour of parents is belligerent, uncooperative, abusive or otherwise disrespectful or overpowering (Boutte et al. 1992). Although at first glance these behaviours can intimidate you, generally the parents feel that they have a valid reason for their behaviour. The notion of collaboration implies that you understand that, from the parents' perspective, their frustration is valid.

The first step to understanding them is not to take their behaviour personally. You will need to deal with their complaints in the same way as you would any other parental complaints. However, you might need to be more assertive than usual in asking them to moderate how they are talking to you.

Heath (1994) advises that you give yourself time to evaluate parents' complaints, rather than immediately agreeing or becoming defensive or apologetic about them. You might need to be more than usually insistent that you will talk with them again about the issue at another time. Take the information, and offer to think about it or gather more facts from another member of staff about the incident in question, and offer to get back to the parents. This gives the parents time to calm down and for you to decide how to respond. A postponement will also avoid having the conflict escalate and will keep you safe from physical abuse or intimidation.

It can also help to remember that anger is only ever the second thing that we feel: it usually follows fear or hurt. This means that instead of getting upset when someone is angry with you, you can notice the feeling that caused the anger, or at least try to understand the other person's perspective. It is true that anger often stems from feeling as if someone has ignored or does not understand our point of view; this is where active listening can be particularly useful because it is simply not as easy for someone to stay angry if the other person really understands our point of view.

Working with parents who seem 'difficult' will be helped when you look at how the issue seems to them. You can also use the assertive skills described earlier in this chapter to demonstrate that you understand their position while stating your own needs or position: 'I realize that sometimes you have to stay late at work. But if you find unexpectedly that you need to stay late, we would appreciate a call so that we can send the children to the after-school-care service to ensure that they are properly supervised until you get here.'

Communicating with parents from non-majority cultures

Just as you plan for the diversity of needs of the children in your care, so too you need to plan to work collaboratively with parents whose needs are atypical. This is more easily done when you already acknowledge that it is not possible or even desirable to work with every parent in the same way (a'Beckett 1988) and so you are willing to respond to all parents as individuals.

Parents who do not speak English have the least access to support from social services. Furthermore, their lack of facility with language denies you the information about their child which would assist you in caring for and educating that child. Informal contacts will be more important than written exchanges for parents who speak but are not confident about reading English. Rather than waiting for difficulties to occur and conferences to become formal, it will help if you can locate a professional translator or invite a community volunteer to accompany non-English speaking parents on a regular basis at drop-off or collection times so that you can pass on day-to-day information about their child's experiences.

Remember that Western culture's focus on individual academic achievement is not common to all cultures (Lopez 1996). Many cultures value social cooperation above competition and social and emotional development over academic success. Therefore, clarify parents' goals for their child's participation in your programme.

When ignorant of parents' cultures, it can be a simple matter just to ask them about the practices in their country. Generally, they do not expect others to know the practices of every country in the world and are glad to explain some of the values which they hold dear. Asking them about their beliefs also avoids assumptions that they will conform to cultural stereotypes.

Rosin (1996b) discusses cultural differences in verbal communication styles and stresses the importance of avoiding jargon and slang when communicating with families. She also reminds us that, 'different ethnic groups interpret non-verbal cues, such as body language, silence, pauses, proximity between speakers, eye contact, and emotional or facial expressions, in different ways' (Rosin 1996b: 21). There is no guaranteed way to avoid the miscommunication that can arise when others misinterpret your body language, but problems can be minimized when you are aware of the potential for crossed wires, check with parents from other cultures what messages they are receiving, and seek some advice about cultural practices from interpreters or other members of a non-majority culture.

Summary

The provision of 'well-placed empathic comments and moral support' is particularly relevant to working with parents whose children have disabilities (Turnbull and Turnbull 1990: 361). Taking the time to listen to parents and accepting how they feel – even when you do not understand *why* – tells them that you accept them for who they are. This can involve listening both to what they say and how they say it.

When you feel that parents and you are working at odds with each other, you can let them know this, but by telling them about you, rather than about themselves. Using the dual skills of listening and assertiveness, then, you can jointly negotiate a solution.

Above all, it is important to treat parents with respect, not only by listening to them, but also by conveying to them information that they need, even if you fear that it could upset them. By passing the information on, you are telling them that you respect their ability to hear it and deal with it. Anything less is patronizing.

The particular communication skill that you employ will depend on who has the problem. If the other person is distressed in some way, then you will listen; if you are being inconvenienced by someone's actions, you will be assertive; if both of you are being inconvenienced, you will use collaborative problem solving. This is summarized in the following box.

Summary of communication skills	
Who owns the problem	**Recommended communication skill**
The parent is upset.	Listening skills.
The teacher's rights or the rights of other children in his/her care are being violated.	Assertiveness skills, followed by listening skills if the parent responds emotionally.
Both the professional and the parent have unmet needs.	Collaboration to find a solution.

Discussion questions

1. What characteristics of your particular environment can make listening to parents difficult for you?
2. Recall a situation where you have needed to communicate something sensitive to parents. What skills contributed to the outcome of your interaction?
3. What adjustment in your communication style have you found that you need to make when speaking with individuals from cultures other than your own?

Chapter 9
Resolving ethical dilemmas in family-centred work

Mothers were not saying that professionals should have no opinions, only that they needed to provide all options in a non-judgemental way in order to allow the families to come to their own conclusions. If asked for personal or professional opinions, providers certainly could give them, but, to be fair, it was important that they base their opinions on current information.

Helm et al. (1998: 60)

Key points

- The provision of human services inevitably involves values and ethics, particularly when professionals work within the context of families.
- Adoption of the family-centred approach means that professionals may work intimately with families and be responsible to many individuals at once.
- Ethical dilemmas occur when professionals have to choose between alternative courses of action, each of which has its own advantages and disadvantages.
- Codes of ethics are used to guide professionals' conduct, although in the main they specify minimum standards of conduct only and offer only very broad guidelines to inform actual practice. These guidelines are not specific and therefore are unlikely to provide the answers to particular ethical dilemmas that professionals will face.

Introduction

Ethics refer to professionals' moral duty and obligation to do what is right, just and good rather than what is merely expedient, convenient or practical (Katz 1995). This chapter is not about the ethics of any particular discipline, however, nor about the general ethical obligations of professionals to individuals, such as the duty of teachers to protect children's freedom to learn and to provide equal opportunities for all (Strike & Soltis

1992). This chapter instead has a wider focus: it will look at the effects of your work not only on the children themselves, but also on their family, because any involvement with children has a wider impact on their family.

A family-centred approach to service provision has implications for the way we conduct ourselves as professionals and how we interact with family members. Specifically, the approach assumes that we will accept individual difference in families, as well as respect family strengths and trust the ability of families to make choices that best serve their interests. It also requires that we respond to families with sensitivity. Most importantly, the family-centred approach assumes that we will direct our efforts towards the family, supporting individuals within the family with the aim of enhancing the functioning of the family group as a whole.

Codes of ethics

A code of ethics is 'a set of statements about appropriate and expected behaviour of members of a professional group' (Stonehouse 1991a: 3) in order that they protect the interests of the people they serve (Sebastian-Nickell and Milne 1992) rather than their own interests (Honey 1991). Ethical principles refer to *how* professionals provide their services and thus such principles augment professionals' obligations to ensure that *what* they do represents best practice.

The Appendix adapts Huber's (1994) code of ethics to family-centred work. It divides guidelines for practitioners into their responsibilities to children, families, colleagues, the community and society, and to themselves as professionals. Such codes may protect recipients of professional services by helping to define professionals' responsibilities to the people to whom they provide a service and guiding professionals in their conduct of that service (Thompson and Rudolph 1996). Codes are a type of contract between recipient and service provider, making professionals accountable for how they conduct themselves (Coady 1991; Corey 1996; Sebastian-Nickell and Milne 1992).

As well as benefiting consumers, codes of ethics also benefit professionals by giving individual practitioners some tools to use when deliberating over ethical dilemmas (Coady 1994; Corey 1996). Sometimes, the code is backed up with legal as well as professional sanctions. However, the law cannot right all wrongs (Coady 1991) and behaving ethically involves far more than behaving legally (Corey 1996). This is because codes of ethics and legislation often specify minimum standards of conduct only, rather than optimal standards. While a particular course of action or approach to service provision may be effective, it could still be illegal or open to criticism because of how it is delivered.

Professional codes of ethics are especially valuable when clients are vulnerable, when the professional is accountable to many different individuals at once, and when judgements about the best course of action cannot rely on evidence but are matters of opinion only.

All three of these features – vulnerable clients, multiple clients and a lack of research evidence – apply especially to working with families and their children with disabilities. The children are often dependent on adults and so cannot escape intrusive or abusive practices; there may be disparities between what services the children, their families, your employer, and the community want you to provide; and there may be little empirical or research evidence about which form of service would be superior.

On the last aspect, Strike and Soltis (1992) give an example of a teacher who refuses to teach a particular topic on the grounds of her assessment that it is beyond the abilities of her students and is giving them negative attitudes towards the subject and to themselves as learners. She has no evidence in the form of, say, self-esteem measures taken before and after the introduction of the unit of study, however, and so in forming her opinion she can only draw on her professional training and experience. Nevertheless, she is qualified to make such a judgement and it is backed up by the spirit – if not the exact letter – of her profession's code of ethics.

Ethical decision-making

Ethical dilemmas arise when two possible courses of action both have benefits and costs, and the professional must choose between them. It is important that such judgements are not arbitrary or capricious (Strike and Soltis 1992). Arbitrary judgements occur when decisions are made without considering all the evidence; capricious decisions are unsystematically formed, without due process (Strike and Soltis 1992).

Two strands must inform your ultimate decision: first, the ideals that underpin professionalism and, second, consideration of the consequences that may arise from your actions (Strike and Soltis 1992).

Ideals

The first, idealistic, approach requires that you behave towards others as you would wish them to act towards you (Strike and Soltis 1992). This approach rests on the principle of equal respect for all persons, which states that all individuals' interests, while different, deserve equal consideration. A shortcoming of this approach to resolving ethical dilemmas is that a high degree of care is necessary to avoid moral arrogance, in which professionals make judgements that stick rigidly to irrational or general principles that are not responsive to individual circumstances (Coady

1994; Strike and Soltis 1992). A second disadvantage is that slavish adherence to general rules discourages practitioners from reflecting on each individual situation, taking each on its merits (Turnbull and Turnbull 1990).

All professions attempt to abide by some basic moral ideals, which are identified by Corey (1996) as the following:

1. *Beneficence* – that is, promoting the good of others.
2. *Non-maleficence* – which means doing no harm.
3. *Autonomy* – which refers to the promotion of independence in others.
4. *Justice* – which refers to giving all those with whom a professional works equal and fair treatment, both in the sense of not discriminating against individuals on the basis of their culture, gender, religion and so on, and in the sense of balancing the rights and interests of one group with those of another group.
5. *Fidelity* – which refers to making honest promises and keeping commitments to others.

Consequences

The consequentialist aspect of decision-making requires you to consider the potential outcomes for all parties, and to choose a course of action which produces better consequences than might otherwise have occurred. However, this assumes that you can predict these future outcomes accurately, which is seldom possible. It also causes us to ignore the need to redress past injustices, as the consequentialist approach focuses entirely on the future.

Conclusion: ethical decision-making

When attempting to resolve ethical dilemmas, you will arrive at a viable set of guidelines by blending ideals with a concern for potential consequences of your actions (Strike & Soltis 1992). Your deliberations will begin by identifying that a dilemma exists and noting the pertinent issues, the individuals involved, and their interests. Then, drawing on your profession's code of practice, your employer's guidelines, and your personal values, you will go through a process of critical reflection in which you check backwards and forwards between your ideals and examination of possible consequences, verifying that your action plan is in tune with your principles and your principles are consistent with your broader goals for the child and family, until you arrive at a decision that you can justify (Coady 1994; Corey 1996; Strike and Soltis 1992). This process is by no means straightforward and your resulting ethical judgement may feel tentative. Nevertheless, having reflected critically on your ideals and the consequences of your decision, you can be confident that your ultimate decision will be rational (Strike and Soltis 1992).

This process should not occur in isolation, however: it is crucial that you discuss the issue with those concerned, as when individuals conduct ethical deliberations in private, they are more likely to assume that their ultimate decision is the only right one, with the result that they will resist alternatives and attempt to impose their decision on others (Strike and Soltis 1992). Instead, when all affected parties contribute equally to a discussion, are in full possession of all relevant facts, and arrive at a consensual opinion, then the resulting decision is more likely to be suitable (Strike and Soltis 1992).

In summary, your ethical choices will be guided by two equally important considerations: your ethical ideals – particularly your concern for fellow human beings and empathy with others – and the potential outcomes of your decision for all concerned (Coady 1994; Strike and Soltis 1992).

Ethical principles

To follow are common principles which have been generated in this way, in the light of potential negative consequences for clients if violations occur, and guided by the ideals of professionalism:

1. Professionals should do no harm.
2. Individuals have the right to competent service from professionals.
3. Professional involvement requires informed consent.
4. Confidentiality for individuals and families must be preserved.
5. Individuals' independence must be supported.
6. Professionals need to work within the constraints of their employing agency.

A discussion of these principles and their implications forms the remainder of this chapter.

Principle 1: Do no harm

A fundamental ethical principle is that professionals must not participate in practices that are disrespectful, degrading, intimidating, psychologically damaging, exploitative, or physically harmful to those to whom they provide services (Australian Early Childhood Association 1991; National Association for the Education of Young Children 1989). Society gives professionals power over the people whom they serve (Sokoly and Dokecki 1995). It is essential, therefore, that we use our influence over others in their best interests and in open consultation with them.

Practical implications of Principle 1

The caveat that professionals avoid harming the people they serve implies that they need to know their own values and motivations. It also means working collaboratively with family members and colleagues.

Self-awareness

Corey (1996) observes that ethical decision making is an evolutionary process that requires professionals to be continually aware of their own values and biases. Therefore, you have a responsibility to be aware of your values, so that they do not interfere with establishing a respectful relationship with the families with whom you work.

Social awareness

Helping does not occur in a vacuum: you will need to be aware of the ecological factors that can bring about individuals' and families' distress (Corey 1996). An example is when a child with special needs is not receiving adequate services, which is causing his or her family to be concerned. Corey (1996) says that professionals might at times need to become active agents of social change; at other times, however, it can be necessary to help family members recognize and act on their options, even when those options arc limited.

Cultural awareness

It is neither ethical nor sound to apply a monocultural model of service delivery in a multicultural society (Corey 1996). Professionals have a responsibility to respect cultural differences, gain knowledge of a range of cultures, be personally aware and sensitive to families from cultural backgrounds that are different from their own, and use culturally relevant practices in their work (Corey 1996). However, it will also be important to remember that cultural groups are not homogeneous and that each family is a unique expression of many characteristics and ecological conditions. Thus, it is important to avoid stereotypes about the impact of non-majority cultures on their members and to consider each family's particular circumstances individually (Roberts et al. 1998).

Your service to and involvement with families should not require families to go against their cultural values and beliefs. An example of an inappropriate requirement may be expecting parents to allow their adolescent son or daughter to live independently, when in their culture a child becomes independent only when he or she marries.

One view of ethics states that all values are relative to their culture and so all cultural practices are equally valid. However, Strike and Soltis (1992) argue that this is clearly not so and that the notion does people a disservice as they do not learn to make moral choices by being told that all practices are equally valid. These writers go on to argue that certain principles (such as those listed here) are fundamental to all persons, regardless of their culture. Cultural differences are often not about differences in values as such, but about different ways of achieving the same outcome, which implies that professionals need to be aware of differing cultural expressions of these common ideals (Coady 1994). This injunction will not satisfy all instances, of course, such as when parents want to deny their child some necessary medical treatment, when this appears in your own culture to constitute neglect.

Assessing whether professional involvement will be beneficial

The aim of working with a family is obviously to serve its interests. However, just by being there, you might be implying some unintended and unhelpful messages about the family's competence. For instance, parents might feel that they have failed, as they need to ask for professional help or they might feel overwhelmed by the number of agencies involved with their child. Therefore, as early as possible, convey your faith in the parents' ability to manage their own family so that their confidence is not undermined. It is important that your eagerness to 'help' does not stifle family members' efforts to help themselves.

A second way in which you can avoid inflicting harm on those families with whom you work is to highlight their strengths rather than any shortcomings. Systems theory accepts that individuals are doing the best they can with the resources that are presently available to them but, as parents might not be aware of their achievements, it can be useful to help them to focus on these.

A third way to avoid harming families is to keep in mind that the principle of normalization applies to them, just as it does to individuals with disabilities. This principle upholds that people should have access to conditions of everyday life that are as close as possible to the usual patterns of society (Hayes 1990). This principle is most often applied to individuals with disabilities but it is clear, for example, that having many professionals working with one's family is not typical. Therefore, as discussed in Chapter 7, it may be helpful to families if you assist them to streamline agency and professional services so they are not overwhelmed by professional involvement.

Maintaining family balance

The injunction to do no harm implies that you must not favour one particular individual within the family, but instead balance the needs of all family members. Professional involvement could unbalance the family, causing individual members to focus on the needs of the child with a disability, to the exclusion of the needs of other family members. In the short term this may be necessary, but in the long term it will be detrimental to each family member and may unbalance the whole family unit.

If you undermine the parents, you will disempower them and make it difficult for them to make executive decisions for their family. To empower parents, it can help if you ask how they would like to use you and your time. In this way, they remain in charge of you (as your symbolic employer) rather than your being in charge of them because of your expertise.

Collaborating with families and colleagues

If you see yourself as working alongside families, you are less likely to do them harm than if you adopt an expert stance. Being an expert adviser is likely to undermine the parents' function as effective family leaders. Collaboration involves defining with family members their goals for your working relationship (Sokoly and Dokecki 1995). This is likely to avoid the misuse of the power that you possess by virtue of your actual or presumed professional expertise.

Collaboration also requires you to work with any other professionals who are involved with the individuals or families whom you are serving to ensure that the services are coordinated, lest disorganization and chaos result. Just as is the case for families, when you collaborate with colleagues it will be important not to adopt a superior position to them.

Also consider that families who are experiencing very difficult times may invite you to take on a leadership role; your own eagerness to help could see you do this quite readily. While taking on a 'key worker' role and liaising with other agencies for families can certainly be useful in some circumstances, it can also help the family if you encourage them to deal directly with the other agencies, rather than being their broker or go-between.

Resisting bias

The fundamental guideline to do no harm implies that you must resist having biases against those with whom you work. The word *bias* has two levels of meaning. The first occurs when professionals are employed by large organizations – such as schools or welfare agencies – that have had prior contact with particular families. Because of this prior contact, professionals can have information about a family before they meet its members. The second level of bias refers to the fact that, based on this information, professionals might make value judgements about a family or pre-judge what their 'problem' is or what services they might need.

Both sorts of bias mean that professionals can be at risk of:

- gathering information that confirms their ideas about the family and disregarding conflicting evidence;
- owning or magnifying the family's difficulties – that is, feeling more uncomfortable about them than the family does;
- wanting therefore to help, which may give family members a message that they cannot cope alone.

This bias leads to ineffective services (see Vignette 1).

Vignette 1

You are a teacher. In the school where you work there is a child who has a reputation for 'wild' and sometimes unusual behaviour. He and his family are regularly the topic of staff room discussions and his parents have been described as 'hippies' and 'dropouts'. You have also heard that the family relies on welfare payments for its income and that neither parent has ever held down a 'real job'. Other staff members complain that the mother never wears shoes and is 'unkempt'. There are also complaints from other teachers that the parents never attend school functions or seem interested in school affairs. You are informed that the child will be in your class in the coming year.

Analysis: The practical implications of Principle 1 are at work here. It is important that you resist bias in your approach to the child and his family. You may need to examine your own values and remember that a family-centred approach requires you to respect all families and focus on family strengths. You may also note that your colleagues may have been biased in making judgements about the family and that their discussions about the family have violated Principle 4 (that confidentiality for individuals and families must be preserved).

In future, you will need to ensure that you do not initiate gossip about any child or family, and tactfully withdraw whenever a named child or family is being discussed in an unprofessional way. Also note that family systems theory would hold that the behaviour of the parents does not exist in a vacuum but is likely to be linked to the reception they have received from the school in the past.

Principle 2: Individuals have the right to competent service from professionals

The second ethical principle is that it is crucial that professionals are sensitive to individuals' rights to freedom and dignity while, at the same time, providing each individual or family with the most effective service (Rekers 1984). To that end, professionals have a responsibility to be competent, which includes:

- knowledge of the theories in their specialty area;
- being trained and experienced in the field in which they are offering a service (Corey 1996);
- ensuring that inexperienced staff members are supervised closely by senior colleagues;
- being aware of instances where their own human frailties could lead to inadequate professional performance that could harm the welfare of those with whom they work (Corey 1996);
- knowledge of the full range of service options or approaches;
- knowledge of services that could be of use to individuals and families and how to refer them to such services;
- being aware of their own personal and professional limitations and referring to specialists if they are not equipped to deal with individual difficulties;
- having exposure to ongoing training;
- ensuring that experienced staff members can consult with colleagues when they are in doubt about their work;
- collaborating with other professionals who are also working with the individuals or families they serve (Geldard 1998).

Coady (1994) draws attention to a profession's temptation to exaggerate what it knows. She states that professionals need to be aware of the limits of their profession's and their own personal knowledge base and, keeping this in mind, advise others with 'due humility' about the correctness of their advice (Coady 1994: 8).

Practical implications of Principle 2

The right to competent service implies that professionals need to document what they are doing to evaluate whether it is effective. Also, they need to ensure that their personal vulnerabilities do not impede competent service provision. Professionals' awareness about their professional and personal limits safeguards both those with whom they work and their ongoing professional growth (Corey 1996).

Ongoing evaluation

Careful documentation of your work with families will enable you to monitor the outcomes and effectiveness of your professional involvement. This makes the entire process visible, understandable and open to evaluation by others, which is the basis of accountability (Alberto and Troutman 1999). As well as monitoring for possible negative effects, this accountability allows you to demonstrate and document your successes and those of the families with whom you work.

Managing stress

You will need to be able to handle the stressors that are involved in your work, so that your own personal stress does not impinge on your ability to be useful to others. This includes taking responsibility for setting up professional and personal support networks to replenish your energies and ensuring that those whom you supervise are also supported in their professional roles (see Vignette 2). You also need to safeguard your own privacy and place limits on your professional relationships and responsibilities to avoid becoming overburdened.

Referral on

A final implication of the duty to offer competent service is that when you cannot provide a service that a family requires, you have a responsibility to find out who can provide that service and to inform families about these other agencies. This involves knowledge of available services, awareness of how to make referrals and, perhaps, attending the first meeting or so with the family, until they feel comfortable about working with a new service provider.

Principle 3: Professional involvement requires informed consent

The third ethical principle is that individuals must consent to professional involvement. Consent relies on three conditions being satisfied: first, that an individual is competent – that is, has the capacity – to consent; second, that the consent is voluntary; and, third, that the individual has sufficient information to guide his or her choice (Rekers 1984). In almost all cases, the parents of a child who has a disability will be competent to consent on their own and their child's behalf. However, the issue of their capacity to consent is not always straight forward:

- When the parents themselves have an intellectual disability, you might question how you can convey information clearly to them, to enable them to give their informed consent.

Vignette 2

A new graduate is employed in an isolated rural education service with minimal supervision. The service deals with students whose behavioural difficulties have caused them to be expelled from other settings. You are a senior staff member who becomes concerned that the new graduate is not receiving supervision in a demanding field of work.

Analysis: Principle 2 (the right to competent service) is being violated by the fact that a new entrant to the profession is being expected to be highly competent in an especially demanding field. As a senior professional, you might bring the situation to the attention of your employer and request a reduction in your own workload to enable you to supervise the new graduate. You might also help the new graduate to establish a network with professionals from other agencies with whom to consult about difficult cases and who can provide some backup in case of crises or in periods when you are not available to supervise the novice yourself.

- What do you do when the parents do not wish to consent to a course of action that you are convinced is in the child's best interests?
- What should happen when the two parents are separated or divorced: do you seek the consent only of the child's guardian or, as many organizations espouse, do you require the consent of both parents? And what happens if you cannot locate one of the parents?

The second condition of Principle 3, *voluntary* consent, requires that no unfair consequences occur if parents withhold consent to a particular practice or programme (Rekers 1984). Further, Alberto and Troutman (1999) affirm that parents who refuse to consent to a particular programme cannot be threatened with no service for their child, and neither can they be promised extravagant benefits if they do participate (see Vignette 3). Furthermore, professionals cannot use emotional blackmail to coerce parents into giving their consent. Norris and Closs (1999: 31) state this principle eloquently: 'Although rarely made explicit, some teachers [seem] to expect families' compliance with school values and practices "in exchange" for the extra effort it [takes] to meet children's needs.'

The third condition, *informed* consent, involves giving people enough information so that they can make a prudent choice about using particular services without, at the same time, overwhelming them with too much detail (Corey 1996).

In order to give their consent, individuals will need to know some or all of the following information (Corey 1996):

- your general goals;
- your responsibilities towards them;
- their responsibilities;
- limits on confidentiality (see the later section on this issue) – such as whether you will be recording, having someone else observe your work, or discussing the individual or his or her family with a supervisor;
- legal constraints on your relationship;
- the risks involved for the individual or family;
- your qualifications;
- the anticipated length of your involvement;
- any fees that are involved.

The issue of informed consent is particularly delicate when those giving their consent have a different cultural background from your own or do not speak the same language as you. Under these conditions it is essential to engage the services of a skilled interpreter. When working with an interpreter, it is important to remember to address the family member rather than the interpreter (Rosin 1996a). It is not appropriate to rely on a sibling (and is less than fair to the sibling) to interpret for parents in matters concerning a child's programme or where consent is required.

Vignette 3

You are a teacher in a special school who works with your students on independence training. The parents of one of your 15-year-old students do not want their son to take part in the transport training component of the programme because they feel that he would be in danger if he lost his way in the community. What should you do?

Analysis: Principle 3 is at work here. In this situation it is essential to respect the parents' position as family leaders and obtain their consent to the programme. On the other hand, Principle 5 (which states that professionals must support individuals' independence) is also at work because, while aware of the risks of transport training, you also believe that your student will benefit from the increased independence it would provide him. You could acknowledge to the parents that there are some risks involved in transport training, explain what steps you plan to take to minimize those risks, and highlight the benefits to the student if he can become more mobile in the community. Nevertheless, in line with Principle 3, you will need to accept the parents' final decision about their son's involvement. This is an example of a situation where many principles are at work but you need to decide which takes precedence.

Practical implications of Principle 3

Your professional status may mean that parents or others are subtly pressured into consenting to your plan of action. Therefore the onus is on you to ensure that what they are agreeing to represents best practice (Rekers 1984) and that a range of viable service options have been fully considered and explored with them (Martin and Pear 1999).

Sometimes, families are pressured by other professionals to receive a service that they do not really want. At other times, your own agency might pressure you into offering a service that the family does not need – for instance, routine case reviews for a child with a disability. In either instance, voluntary consent is compromised, resulting in an ethical dilemma which requires resolution before you proceed any further.

It is important that teachers gain parental consent if their intended involvement with a child is beyond the realms of what would ordinarily be considered to be part of their teaching role. For example, if a teacher intended to implement an intensive behaviour management programme with a child, he or she would usually involve the parents in its planning and gain consent for its implementation. It is also important that teachers gain the written consent of parents if they intend to request formal assessments or enlist the assistance of consultant professionals such as psychologists or other specialists.

Principle 4: Confidentiality for individuals and families must be preserved

The fourth ethical principle states that people have a right to choose who knows personal information about them, especially when that information could be used to discriminate against them (Coady 1994). This is the principle of privacy (Thompson and Rudolph 1996).

Confidentiality is a related principle that refers to professionals' responsibility to respect privacy and to limit who has access to personal information about the individuals and families with whom they work (Thompson and Rudolph 1996). Confidentiality is central to establishing a trusting and effective professional relationship (Corey 1996).

Four ethical principles are involved in professionals' duty to protect confidentiality (Coady 1994): These are their duties to:

1. respect the autonomy of the individuals and families they serve;
2. keep the implied promise not to disclose private information;
3. respect relationships and the trust that is inherent in them;
4. avoid harm to those whom they serve (Coady 1994).

There is also a pragmatic or 'prudential' reason to maintain confidentiality (Coady 1994: 7). This reason is that people are unlikely to disclose information that professionals need to do their job effectively, unless they can trust professionals to keep that information confidential.

In practice, confidentiality involves taking action to:

- safeguard personal files or other records;
- keep these records accurate, unbiased and fair;
- avoid staff room gossip about particular children and families;
- make available to individuals all the information in their files.

Labels can defy the confidentiality ethic also, because they often define people negatively, even when 'dressed up' in professional terms, such as when we define parents as being in denial about their child's disability, or as being enmeshed, over-involved, or chaotic, to name but a few terms. These labels and the more formal diagnostic labels – such as 'personality disordered' – not only violate confidentiality when we describe individuals in this way to others, but they also display a lack of respect for them.

Limits on confidentiality

The requirement to maintain confidentiality is not absolute. The following are some ethical reasons to limit confidentiality (Coady 1994; Geldard 1998).

Freedom of information

At the request of individuals, their information can be released to themselves or to someone whom they nominate (Corey 1996).

Multi-disciplinary teams

Professionals who work as part of multi-disciplinary teams often share relevant information to ensure that each has sufficient knowledge of a child's or family's circumstances to be of use to them. Staff who team-teach or work in trans- or multi-disciplinary teams will frequently need to exchange information with other professionals who are working with the same child or family so that the family can receive services that reflect their needs. This kind of information exchange for professional purposes, however, is in contrast with gossip, which passes on information to people who do not need to know it, and often in a disrespectful way. It is also important that parents consent to and are aware of the sharing of information both within and between multi-disciplinary teams.

Threats of harm

Information cannot be kept confidential when an individual threatens to harm him- or herself or another person (Corey 1996). This reflects professionals' double duty to protect other people from potential danger and to take all reasonable steps to prevent those with whom they work from harming themselves (Corey 1996). (This principle reflects the fact that professionals have responsibilities to the community as well as to those whom they directly serve.)

Child abuse or neglect

All health and education professionals have a responsibility to report suspected instances of child abuse. Across the USA, Canada and Australia, this responsibility is mandated by law; in the UK, professionals are not legally obliged to report their suspicions, although the HMSO guideline is that they 'should' do so. Some professionals are reluctant to do so on the grounds that more harm may be caused to the child concerned (Coady 1994); despite this possibility, if you are a mandated notifier of child abuse and neglect, you are still *obliged* by law to notify the local child welfare authority regarding the suspected abuse or neglect of any child with whom you come into contact.

Employer policy

A school or service agency might have a policy which requires practitioners to disclose students' illegal conduct – such as illicit drug use – to authorities and/or the students' parents.

Legal requirements

When a matter has come before a court, professionals will be obliged to disclose otherwise confidential information that relates to their involvement with individuals or families involved in the case.

Practical implication of Principle 4

At the outset of your relationship with individuals and families, it will be important to tell them the situations in which you might have to disclose otherwise confidential information that they have told you. If you need to coordinate your services with other professionals inside or outside of your organization, there will be times when you need to pass on to them information about a child or family with whom you are working. You will need to gain consent to do this and ensure that the family remains in charge and knows what each professional is being told about them (see Vignette 4). Their consent may be restricted – for example, when they consent to your sharing information concerning the details of their child's speech and language assessment but not those concerning their negotiations for custody of the child.

Vignette 4

You are a teacher and one of your students has significant behavioural difficulties. His parents have discussed the child's behaviour with you and indicated that they are seeking assistance from a community based team as his behaviour is becoming increasingly difficult to manage at home. The psychologist from this team phones you at school and requests information about the child's classroom behaviour.

Analysis: Principle 4 (the right to confidentiality) is at work here. Even though the parents have informed you about the team's involvement and it is likely that collaboration between all professionals involved with the child will benefit him and his family, you have not yet been authorized to discuss the child or his classroom behaviour with the members of this team. However, you can respectfully explain your position to the psychologist, inform the parents of the request and seek their consent before discussing their child with the psychologist.

Where you have the appropriate consent, you can involve parents in communications in which you disclose information about them by writing letters to other professionals in collaboration with the family and then giving them copies of those letters. You can invite them to attend a case conference in which the team will be discussing their child, or help a child to tell his or her parents information that otherwise you would be obliged to report to the parents yourself. (There is an exception to this guideline in cases of child sexual abuse, when you ordinarily would not disclose to a suspected perpetrator that you are making a report of the suspected abuse, as that could give the perpetrator time to make up a plausible answer to the allegations.)

Principle 5: Support individuals' independence

The fifth principle of ethical professional conduct relates to when families request support. The principle of promoting the independence of others upholds that it is important to balance providing a service to people who are in need while, at the same time, not creating dependency or undermining family members' awareness of their own skills and strengths. As professionals often deal with families at times of crisis, we run the risk of being seen by the families as 'rescuing' them, while they see themselves as 'helpless' or needy and unable to solve their own problems.

Your own needs

Your professional relationships with individuals and families exist for their benefit, not yours (Corey 1996). While it is self-evident that many people enter the helping professions in order to help people, you will need to be aware of your own motivation so that your desire to help others does not keep them dependent on you (Corey 1996). Your authority as an effective professional is a powerful quality, but there is also the potential for it to be detrimental to others when they become reliant on it (Corey 1996) and detrimental to yourself when your own self-esteem is dependent on it.

Carmen Berry (1988) talks of Messiahs or 'helpaholics' who habitually set up one-up/one-down relationships. These people help others, but mainly to satisfy their own needs for nurturing and affection (bought through others' gratitude and admiration), rather than because the recipients need help (Berry 1988; Corey 1996). Relationships in which there is a power imbalance between the partners can undermine the skills of the person being 'helped', and will eventually overwhelm the helpaholic, as Berry (1988: 56–57) describes:

> Feelings of inadequacy and powerlessness, obligation and rage motivate the Messiah. Being a 'helpaholic' can be just as addictive, compulsive and destructive as any other addiction . . . Messiahs do good things for the wrong reasons, and therefore the best of their efforts prove futile.

Family members' needs

Dependency is seldom an issue with teaching; however, it is a challenging problem in the professions that deliver a clinical service to children or families. In these instances, dependency has three aspects. The first is when family members do not want to end their relationship with you, even when they no longer need your involvement. Especially if you have worked together for some time, it will require sensitivity and tact to give families the confidence to resume independent control of their lives.

A second issue is when the family continues to need a service, but you are not able to continue working with them. In this case, you have a responsibility to refer them to another practitioner. It might help vulnerable individuals if you offer to attend with them at the first appointment with the new practitioner, to give them the confidence to move on to the new service.

A third dilemma arises when you have successfully withdrawn your involvement with a family, but a colleague becomes concerned about them and wants you to make contact again. This can be a particular issue when you are working in a trans- or multi-disciplinary team. The dilemma with resuming contact is that it implies that the family cannot manage its own day-to-day ups and downs without professional help. To imply this would promote their dependence on professionals. Therefore, when you believe that a family does not need your involvement, you could explain your judgement and discuss what has to happen for your colleague to feel satisfied that the family can be independent.

Practical implications of Principle 5

Principle 5 requires that professional relationships support the independence of those served. It requires that professionals avoid personal relationships with the people whom they are serving and that they place limits on the relationship to enable individuals to maintain their autonomy.

Avoid dual relationships with families

Professional relationships have an agenda: the professional wants to assist the family in some way. In contrast, friendships do not have any agenda. Thus, personal relationships with the people you serve can exploit them and confuse you both about your roles (Corey 1996). This means that in your work, you can be friendly and warm while not necessarily being a 'friend' to the people whom you are serving (see Vignette 5).

Sexual relationships between professionals and those they serve are particularly inappropriate, even if the other person consents. Sexual relationships have the potential to cause real harm by violating the special trust that individuals place in professionals and by increasing their dependence on the professional relationship. This violation is akin to incest (Pope 1988). While it is possible that during your working life you might feel personally or sexually attracted to some individuals, there is a crucial distinction between feeling these emotions and acting on them (Corey 1996).

Vignette 5

You are a member of a multi-disciplinary team attached to a school district and have begun a close non-romantic friendship with the parent of a child to whom you are providing a service. You and the parent spend considerable time together in your off-duty time, while you remain part of the team who is responsible for providing a service to the child and her family.

Analysis: Principle 5 is being violated here. Your own needs for friendship are being met at the expense of the child and parent over whom you have some power. A dual relationship is in progress. You will need to terminate the relationship with the parent for as long as you continue to be professionally involved with the family. If neither of you wants this, you could remove the family from your caseload as long as you can refer them on to another team member. Or, you could move to another workplace to avoid exploitation or impairment of your professional judgement.

On the other hand, Corey (1996) also says that it is sometimes not possible to maintain a single role in professional work. For instance, if you work in a rural community, the individuals with whom you work can also be members of your church or some other social group (Corey 1996). There are also times when it is not desirable to avoid dual relationships, such as when interacting with individuals in informal ways can be more effective than formal meetings. Nevertheless, in these cases, you will need to give careful thought to how you will manage the complexities involved in dual relationships – specifically how you can avoid exploiting the people with whom you work.

Limit the professional relationship

A second implication of the principle that professionals must promote the independence of the people with whom they work is that they must place limits on the professional relationship (Rogers 1942). He argued if professionals allow demands from those they serve to escalate, the burden can become overwhelming to the point where affection and the desire to help can turn into avoidance and dislike (Rogers 1942). The modern terms for this syndrome are 'burnout' or 'compassion fatigue'. At the same time, people will feel rejected and betrayed if you offer a service that you later cannot sustain. For this reason, it will be important to negotiate the limits of your work, so that you both agree on the form of your working relationship.

Some organizations use written contracts for this purpose. Mostly, however, a request for an inappropriate form of help will arise unexpectedly. If a parent asks you to do something that is outside of your role – such as when she asks you, her son's teacher, to take him to school as she cannot do this herself, then one option is to ask the parent who else she would have contacted if you had been unavailable. The two of you can then generate a more appropriate plan that meets the parent's needs without imposing unrealistically on you.

Principle 6: Work within agency constraints

The sixth ethical principle of professional conduct is that when deciding whether to become involved with a family, you need to know that the services you want to offer are within your role and field of expertise, and are endorsed by your employer (see Vignette 6).

Practical implications of Principle 6

Principle 6 addresses some of the constraints under which you function and your responsibility to your employer. Limits are inevitable.

Vignette 6

You teach in a regular school that is attended by some children with disabilities. A parent of a disabled child in your class begins talking with you about the difficulties of managing her child's caretaking needs. This soon develops into repeated conversations about her marital problems. In other words, she wants you to help her, not her child. What should you do?

Analysis: As a teacher, it is not your role to provide marital counselling to parents. Your employer would not support this use of your time. Therefore, Principle 6 is at issue here. (Also, unless you are trained in marital counselling, Principle 2 – the right to competent service – is also an issue.) Furman (1995) suggests clarifying your role as sensitively as you can, perhaps by asking the mother how the two parents are managing to protect the child from their marital problems. This clarifies that your primary concern is the child's welfare. Next, you could ask the mother whether she would like the name of a counsellor whom you could recommend.

Advocate for improved policy

Large organizational structures can sometimes leave professionals feeling powerless. They may feel that the 'system' prevents them from working in the way they would like. Nevertheless, Corey and colleagues (1988) caution against avoiding responsibility and blaming the 'system' for your failure to deliver an ethical or high-quality service. Instead, you can assume some power within your organization by advocating for small but useful changes in policy, learning the reasons for your organization's policies, and ordering your personal priorities so that you can decide which compromises you can make without sacrificing your professional integrity. In the meantime, you must abide by the policies of your employer so that you do not compromise yourself and the recipients of your services by promising a service which you are later obliged to withdraw.

Allocate limited resources wisely

An implication of the requirement to place limits on your professional relationships is that you will need to be clear about your area of responsibility. It is unwise to allow yourself to get side-tracked on to other issues that are not within your domain. Your employer will not support you if you are offering a service that is outside of your job description, especially if it does not work out well; it will not be the wisest use of your skills and resources; and it could harm the family. Instead, refer families on to other professionals who specialize in offering the type of service they require.

A second implication is that you must work within your organization's resources. Most agencies have limited resources, with the result that they have to balance the needs of those they serve against the need to use agency resources efficiently. The ideal service for a particular family can be too expensive for the organization to be able to provide while still maintaining its other services. This reality will require you to refer back to the guidelines to balance the needs of one against the needs of many.

Summary

This chapter has described some ethical dilemmas that can arise out of your responsibility to the family members with whom you work. Other dilemmas occur as a result of your responsibilities to trainees whom you are supervising, your school, and your profession. These are listed in the Appendix.

You have an ethical obligation to address the professional and ethical dilemmas that arise in your work (Corey 1996). Although ideal answers to these dilemmas may not be easy to find, rational answers *are* possible, some better and some worse than others (Coady 1994). Your ultimate decisions will draw on your professional ideals as well as an assessment of the potential consequences of your actions.

Discussion questions

1. Does your profession have a code of ethics? If so, how useful is it in guiding day-to-day practice?
2. What are your own personal ideals, both with respect to the children with whom you work and their families?
3. Do you and others at your workplace have sufficient resources and support to ensure that you are able to deliver a competent service?
4. How does your workplace safeguard the confidentiality of children and families?

Appendix
A proposed code of ethics for family-centred work

(adapted from Huber 1994)

Responsibilities to children and families

Principle 1: Do no harm

With respect to my responsibilities to the children with whom I work and their families, I will:

1.1 promote and uphold the provision of high-quality services for all people.

1.2 respect the legal rights of those persons seeking my assistance.

1.3 make reasonable efforts to ensure that my services are used appropriately.

1.4 not discriminate against or refuse professional service to anyone on the basis of race, gender, religion, national origin, or sexual orientation. I respect each person's individual needs, values and culture.

1.5 strive to develop positive relationships with families that are based on mutual trust and open communication.

1.6 encourage families to share their knowledge of their child in order to meet the child's and the family's needs.

1.7 acknowledge families' existing strengths and competence as a basis for supporting them in their task of nurturing their child.

Principle 2: Professional competence and integrity

I will maintain high standards of professional competence and integrity. To that end, I will:

2.1 abide by my profession's code of ethics.

2.2 seek appropriate professional assistance for my personal problems or conflicts that could impair my work performance or judgement.

2.3 be dedicated to high standards of scholarship and will present accurate information.

2.4 base my work on the best theoretical and practical knowledge currently available and keep abreast of research and legislative changes that relate to my professional roles.

2.6 not attempt to diagnose, treat, or advise on problems that are outside the recognized boundaries of my competence.

2.7 collaborate with colleagues and other professionals.

2.8 accept responsibility and accountability for my actions.

2.9 work within the statutory boundaries determined by government legislation.

2.10 not engage in sexual or other harassment or exploitation of clients, students, trainees, supervisees, employees, colleagues or research participants.

Principle 3: Consent

I am aware that consent to service must be voluntary and informed. To ensure this, I will:

3.1 provide clients with complete and accurate information regarding available services.

3.2 not coerce parents into giving their consent by threatening discontinuation of service if consent is withheld, or by promising exorbitant benefits for receiving a service.

3.3 obtain informed consent from clients before videotaping, audio recording, or permitting third party observation.

Principle 4: Confidentiality

I aim to safeguard the privacy of the people with whom I work. Thus, I will:

4.1 hold in confidence any information obtained in my professional capacity and use my professional judgement in sharing such information with colleagues.

4.2 not disclose client confidences except: (a) as mandated by law; (b) to prevent a clear and immediate danger to a person or persons; (c) where I am a defendant in a civil, criminal, or disciplinary action arising from my work (in which case client confidences will be disclosed only in the course of that action); or (d) if there is a waiver previously obtained in writing, and then such information may be revealed only in accordance with the terms of the waiver.

4.3 use client and/or case materials in teaching, writing, and public presentations only if clients consent, and when appropriate steps have been taken to protect client identity and confidentiality.

4.4 store or dispose of client records in ways that maintain confidentiality.

Principle 5: Support clients' independence

I am aware of my potentially influential position with respect to clients, and will avoid exploiting their trust and dependency. Therefore, I will:

5.1 make every effort to avoid dual relationships with clients that could impair my judgment or increase the risk of exploitation of them. Examples of such dual relationships include, but are not limited to, business or close personal relationships with clients. Sexual intimacy with clients is prohibited.

5.2 not use my professional relationships with clients to further my own interests.

5.3 respect the right of clients to make decisions and help them to understand the consequences of these decisions.

5.4 continue a helping relationship only as long as it is reasonably clear that clients are benefiting from the relationship.

5.5 help the people with whom I work to obtain other services if I am unable or unwilling, for appropriate reasons, to provide professional help.

5.6 facilitate self-advocacy skills, and negotiate and advocate on behalf of clients when necessary.

Principle 6: Operate within my role

I am aware of my role and will abide by my employer's priorities for my work. Therefore, I will:

6.1 attempt to resolve organizational constraints on ideal working practices.

6.2 make every attempt to identify and secure appropriate services for individuals who need a service that is outside my role or specialty, or beyond the mandate of my employer.

Responsibility to the profession

I respect the rights and responsibilities of my colleagues to participate in activities that advance the goals of the profession. I will:

1 remain accountable to the standards of the profession when acting as a member or employee of organizations.
2 initiate, participate in, and facilitate research within the scope of my professional roles.
3 participate in activities that contribute to a better community and society, including devoting a portion of my professional activity to services for which there is little or no financial return.
4 encourage public participation in the design and delivery of professional services and in the regulation of practitioners.

Responsibility to students, employees, and supervisees

I am aware of my influential position with respect to students, employees, and supervisees and will not exploit their trust and dependency. To that end, I will:

1 participate in the education and training of students and co-professionals.
2 make every effort to avoid dual relationships that could impair my professional judgement or increase the risk of exploitation of my students, employees or supervisees. When a dual relationship cannot be avoided, I will take appropriate professional precautions to ensure that my judgment is not impaired and no exploitation occurs. Examples of such dual relationships include, but are not limited to, business or close personal relationships with students, employees, or supervisees. Provision of therapy to students, employees, or supervisees is prohibited. Sexual intimacy with students or supervisees is prohibited.
3 not permit students, employees, or supervisees to hold themselves out as competent to perform professional services beyond their training, level of experience, and competence.
4 not disclose supervisee confidences except: (a) as mandated by law; (b) to prevent a clear and immediate danger to a person or persons; (c) in educational or training settings where there are multiple supervisors, and then only to other professional colleagues who share responsibility for the training of the supervisee; or (d) if there is a waiver previously obtained in writing, and then such information may be revealed only in accordance with the terms of the waiver.

Financial arrangements

If I function as a private practitioner, I will:

1 disclose my fees to clients at the beginning of services.
2 not offer or accept payment for referrals.
3 not charge excessive fees for services.
4 accurately describe the services that I have rendered and charge only for those services.

Bibliography

a'Beckett C (1988) Parent/staff relationships. In Stonehouse A (Ed) Trusting Toddlers: Programming for One to Three Year Olds in Child Care Centres. Watson, ACT: Australian Early Childhood Association. pp. 140–53.

Abbott CF, Gold S (1991) Conferring with parents when you're concerned that their child needs special services. Young Children, 46(4): 10–14.

Abbott D, Meredith W (1986) Strengths of parents with retarded children. Family Relations 35(3): 371–75.

Alberto PA, Troutman AC (1999) Applied Behavior Analysis for Teachers. 5th edn. Upper Saddle River, NJ: Merrill.

Alper S, Schloss PJ, Schloss CN (1995) Families of children with disabilities in elementary and middle school: Advocacy models and strategies. Exceptional Children 62(3): 261–70.

Anderegg ML, Vergason GA, Smith MC (1992) A visual representation of the grief cycle for use by teachers with families of children with disabilities. Remedial and Special Education 13(2): 17–23.

Andersson B-E (1989) Effects of public day-care – A longitudinal study. Child Development 60(4): 857–66.

Andersson B-E (1992) Effects of day care on cognitive and socioemotional competence of thirteen-year-old Swedish schoolchildren. Child Development 63(1): 20–36.

Appleton PL, Minchom PE (1991) Models of parent partnership and child development centres. Child Care and Health Development 17: 27–38.

Arthur L, Beecher B, Dockett S, Farmer S, Death E (1996) Programming and Planning in Early Childhood Settings. 2nd edn. Sydney: Harcourt Brace.

Australian Early Childhood Association (1991) Australian Early Childhood Association code of ethics. Australian Journal of Early Childhood 16(1): 3–6.

Avila D, Combs A, Purkey W (1977) The Helping Relationship Sourcebook. 2nd edn. Boston, MA: Allyn and Bacon.

Bailey DB, Blasco PM, Simeonsson RJ (1992) Needs expressed by mothers and fathers of young children with disabilities. American Journal on Mental Retardation 97(1): 1–10.

Bailey DB, Buysse V, Palsha SA (1990a) Self-ratings of professional knowledge and skills in early intervention. The Journal of Special Education 23(4): 423–35.

Bailey DB, McWilliam RA, Darkes LA, Hebbeler K, Simeonsson RJ, Spiker D, Wagner M (1998) Family outcomes in early intervention: A framework for program evaluation and efficacy research. Exceptional Children 64(3): 313–28.

179

Bailey DB, Palsha SA, Simeonsson RJ (1991) Professional skills, concerns, and perceived importance of work with families in early intervention. Exceptional Children 58(2): 156–65.

Bailey DB, Simeonsson RJ, Yoder DE, Huntington GS (1990b) Preparing professionals to serve infants and toddlers with handicaps and their families: An integrative analysis across eight disciplines. Exceptional Children 57(1): 26–35.

Bailey DB, Wolery M (1992) Teaching Infants and Preschoolers with Disabilities. 2nd edn. Columbus, OH: Merrill.

Bakken J, Mitlenberger RG, Schauss S (1993) Teaching parents with mental retardation: Knowledge versus skills. American Journal on Mental Retardation 97(4): 405–17.

Baltes P (1987) Theoretical propositions of life-span developmental psychology: On the dynamics between growth and decline. Developmental Psychology 23(5): 611–26.

Barnett WS, Boyce GC (1995) Effects of children with Down Syndrome on parents' activities. American Journal on Mental Retardation 100(2): 115–27.

Baxter C (1987) Professional services as support: Perceptions of parents. Australia and New Zealand Journal of Developmental Disabilities 13(4): 243–53.

Baxter C (1989) Parental access to assistance from services: Social status and age-related differences. Australia and New Zealand Journal of Developmental Disabilities 15(1): 15–25.

Baydar N, Brookes-Gunn J (1998) Profiles of grandmothers who help care for their grandchildren in the United States. Family Relations 47(4): 385–93.

Beckman PJ (1991) Comparison of mothers' and fathers' perceptions of the effect of young children with and without disabilities. American Journal on Mental Retardation 95(5): 585–95.

Begun AL (1996) Family systems and family-centred care. In Rosin P, Whitehead AD, Tuchman LI, Jesien GS, Begun AL, Irwin L, (Eds) Partnerships in Family-Centred Care: A Guide to Collaborative Early Intervention. Baltimore, MD: Paul H Brookes. pp. 33–64.

Behr SK, Murphy DL (1993) Research progress and promise: The role of perceptions in cognitive adaptation to disability. In Turnbull AP, Patterson JM, Behr SK, Murphy DL, Marquis JG, Blue-Banning MJ, (Eds) Cognitive coping, families and disability. Baltimore, MD: Paul H Brookes. pp. 151–63.

Bell MB, Smith BR (1996) Grandparents as primary caregivers: Lessons in love. Teaching Exceptional Children 28(2): 18–19.

Bennett AT (1988) Gateways to powerlessness: Incorporating Hispanic deaf children and families into formal schooling. Disability, Handicap and Society 3(2): 121–51.

Bennett T, Lee H, Lueke B (1998) Expectations and concerns: What mothers and fathers say about inclusion. Education and Training in Mental Retardation and Developmental Disabilities 33(2): 108–22.

Benson BA, Gross AM (1989) The effect of a congenitally handicapped child on the marital dyad. Clinical Psychology Review 9: 747–58.

Bentley-Williams R, Butterfield N (1996) Transition from early intervention to school: A family focussed view of the issues involved. Australasian Journal of Special Education 20(2): 17–28.

Bernard C (1999) Child sexual abuse and the Black disabled child. Disability and Society 14(3): 325–39.

Berry C (1988) When Helping You is Hurting Me. San Francisco, CA: Harper and Row.

Berry JO, Hardman ML (1998) Lifespan Perspectives on the Family and Disability. Boston, MA: Allyn and Bacon.

Blackard MK, Barsch ET (1982) Parents' and professionals' perceptions of the handicapped child's impact on the family. TASH Journal 7: 62–70.

Bland LC, Sowa CJ, Callahan CM (1994) Overview of resilience in gifted children. Roeper Review 17(2): 77–80.

Blodgett H (1971) Mentally Retarded Children: What Parents and Others Should Know. Minneapolis, MN: University of Minnesota.

Bolton R (1987) People Skills. Sydney: Simon and Schuster.

Booth T, Booth W (1995) Unto us a child is born: The trials and rewards of parenthood for people with learning difficulties. Australia and New Zealand Journal of Developmental Disabilities 20(1): 25–39.

Bottomley G (1983) Review of historical and sociological models of the family. In Burns A, Bottomley G, Jools P, (Eds) 'The Family' in the Modern World. Sydney: Allen and Unwin. pp. 3–18.

Botuck S, Winsberg BG (1991) Effects of respite on mothers of school age and adult children with severe disabilities. Mental Retardation 29(1): 43–47.

Boutte GS, Keepler DL, Tyler VS, Terry BZ (1992) Effective techniques for involving 'difficult' parents. Young Children 47(3): 19–22.

Branson J, Miller D, Branson K (1988) An obstacle race: A case study of a child's schooling in Australia and England. Disability, Handicap and Society 3(2): 101–18.

Bright RW, Wright JMC (1986) Community-based services The impact on mothers of children with disabilities. Australia and New Zealand Journal of Developmental Disabilities 12(4): 223–28.

Brinker RP, Seifer R, Sameroff A J (1994) Relations among maternal stress, cognitive development, and early intervention in middle- and low-SES infants with developmental disabilities. American Journal on Mental Retardation 98(4): 463–80.

Bronfenbrenner U (1977) Toward an experimental ecology of human development. American Psychologist 32(7): 513–31.

Brownlee H (1990) Measuring Living Standards. Melbourne: Australian Institute of Family Studies.

Burns A, Goodnow J (1985) Children and Families in Australia. 2nd edn. Sydney: Allen and Unwin.

Butterworth D (1991) The challenge of day care: Liberation or constraint? Australian Journal of Early Childhood 16(2): 20–23.

Caldwell BM, Guze, SB (1960) A study of the adjustment of parents and siblings of institutionalized and non-institutionalized retarded children. American Journal on Mental Deficiency 64: 845–61.

Cameron SJ, Snowdon A, Orr RR (1992) Emotions experienced by mothers of children with developmental disabilities. Children's Health Care 21(2): 96–102.

Carter EA, McGoldrick M (Eds) (1980) The Family Life Cycle: A Framework for Family Therapy. New York: Gardner Press.

Caughey C (1991) Becoming the child's ally – observations in a classroom for children who have been abused. Young Children 46(4): 22–28.

Cavanagh J, Ashman AF (1985) Stress in families with handicapped children. Australia and New Zealand Journal of Developmental Disabilities 11(3): 151–56.

Child Care Task Force (1996) Interim Report: Future Child Care Provision in Australia. Canberra: Australian Government Publishing Service.

Coady M (1991) Ethics, laws and codes. Australian Journal of Early Childhood 16(1): 17–20.

Coady M (1994) Ethical and legal issues for early childhood practitioners. In Mellor EJ, Coombe KM (Eds) Issues in Early Childhood Services: Australian Perspectives. Dubuque, IO: William C Brown. pp. 1–10.

Coleman M (1991) Planning for the changing nature of family life in schools for young children. Young Children 46(4): 15–20.

Compas BE (1987) Coping with stress during childhood and adolescence. Psychological Bulletin 101(3): 393–403.

Conway RNF (1994) Abuse and intellectual disability: A potential link or inescapable reality? Australia and New Zealand Journal of Developmental Disabilities 19(3): 165–71.

Cook R, Tessier A, Klein D (2000) Adapting Early Childhood Curricula for Children in Inclusive Settings. 5th edn. Englewood Cliffs, NJ: Merrill.

Coots JJ (1998) Family resources and parent participation in schooling activities for their children with developmental delays. The Journal of Special Education 31(4): 498–520.

Corey G (1996) Theory and Practice of Counseling and Psychotherapy. 5th edn. Pacific Grove, CA: Brookes/Cole.

Corey G, Corey MS, Callanan P (1988) Issues and Ethics in the Helping Professions. 3rd edn. Pacific Grove, CA: Brooks/Cole.

Cramer S, Erzkus A, Mayweather K, Pope K, Roeder J, Tone T (1997) Connecting with siblings. Teaching Exceptional Children 30(1): 46–51.

Cunningham C (1985) Training and educational approaches for parents of children with special needs. British Journal of Medical Psychology 58: 285–305.

Daka-Mulwanda V, Thornburg KR, Klein T (1995) Collaboration of services for children and families: A synthesis of recent research and recommendations. Family Relations 44(2): 219–23.

Dale N (1996) Working with Families of Children with Special Needs: Partnership and Practice. London: Routledge.

Deiner PL (1998) Resources for Teaching Children with Diverse Abilities: Birth through Eight. 2nd edn. Fort Worth, TX: Harcourt Brace College Publishers.

Dempsey I (1994) Parental empowerment: An achievable outcome of the National Disability Service Standards. Australian Disability Review 1(94): 21–31.

Deslandes R, Royer E, Potvin P, Leclerc D (1999) Patterns of home and school partnership for general and special education students at secondary level. Exceptional Children 65(4): 496–506.

Dunst CJ (1985) Rethinking early intervention. Analysis and Intervention in Developmental Disabilities 5: 165–201.

Dunst CJ, Johanson C, Trivette CM, Hamby D (1991) Family-oriented early intervention practices: Family-centred or not? Exceptional Children 58(2): 115–26.

Dunst CJ, Trivette C, Deal A (1988) Enabling and Empowering Families: Principles and Guidelines for Practice. Cambridge, MA: Brookline Books.

Dunst CJ, Trivette C, Deal A (1994) Supporting and Strengthening Families: Volume 1: Methods, Strategies, and Practices. Cambridge, MA: Brookline Books.

Dyson LL (1991) Families of young children with handicaps: Parental stress and family functioning. American Journal on Mental Retardation 95(6): 623–29.

Dyson LL (1993) Response to the presence of a child with disabilities: Parental stress and family functioning over time. American Journal on Mental Retardation 98(2): 207–18.

Dyson LL (1997) Fathers and mothers of school-age children with developmental disabilities: Parental stress, family functioning, and social support. American Journal on Mental Retardation 102(3): 267–79.

Erickson M, Upshur CC (1989) Caretaking burden and social support: Comparison of mothers of infants with and without disabilities. American Journal on Mental Retardation 94(3): 250–58.

Fantuzzo JW, Wray L, Hall R, Goins C, Azar, S (1986) Parent and social-skills training for mentally retarded mothers identified as child maltreaters: American Journal on Mental Deficiency 91(2): 135–140.

Feldman MA (1994) Parenting education for parents with intellectual disabilities: A review of outcome studies. Research in Developmental Disabilities 15(4): 299–332.

Feldman MA, Case L, Garrick M, MacIntyre-Grande W, Carnwell J, Sparks B (1992) Teaching child-care skills to mothers with developmental disabilities. Journal of Applied Behavior Analysis 25(1): 205–15.

Feldman MA, Case L, Rincover A, Towns F, Betel J (1989) Parent education project III: Increasing affection and responsivity in developmentally handicapped mothers: Component analysis, generalization, and effects on child language. Journal of Applied Behavior Analysis 22(2): 211–22.

Feldman MA, Towns F, Betel J, Case L, Rincover A, Rubino CA (1986) Parent education project II: Increasing stimulating interactions of developmentally handicapped mothers. Journal of Applied Behavior Analysis 19(1): 23–37.

Field T (1991) Quality infant day-care and grade school behavior and performance. Child Development 62(4): 863–70.

Field T, Masi W, Goldestein S, Perry S, Parl S (1988) Infant day care facilitates preschool social behavior. Early Childhood Research Quarterly 3: 341–59.

Fleet A, Clyde M (1993) What's in a Day? Working in Early Childhood. Wentworth Falls, NSW: Social Science Press.

Foster M, Berger M, McLean M (1981) Rethinking a good idea: A reassessment of parent involvement. Topics in Early Childhood Special Education 1(3): 55–65.

Frank N, Newcomb S, Beckman PJ (1996) Developing and implementing support groups for families. In Beckman PJ, (Ed) Strategies for Working with Families of Young Children with Disabilities. Baltimore, MD: Paul H Brookes. pp.127–149.

Freeman SFN, Alkin MC, Kasari CL (1999) Satisfaction and desire for change in educational placement for children with Down Syndrome: perceptions of parents. Remedial and Special Education 20(3): 143–51.

Frey J (1984) A family/systems approach to illness-maintaining behaviors in chronically ill adolescents. Family Process 23(2): 251–60.

Frey KS, Fewell RR, Vadasy PF (1989) Parental adjustment and changes in child outcome among families of young handicapped children. Topics in Early Childhood Special Education 8(4): 38–57.

Friend M, Cook L (1996) Interactions: Collaboration Skills for School Professionals. 2nd edn. New York: Longman.

Fujiura GT (1998) Demography of family households. American Journal on Mental Retardation 103(3): 225–35.

Furman RA (1995) Helping children cope with stress and deal with feelings. Young Children 50(2): 33–41.

Galinsky E (1989) A parent/teacher study: Interesting results. Young Children 45(1): 2–3.

Galinsky E (1990) Why are some parent/teacher partnerships clouded with difficulties? Young Children 45(5): 2-3; 38–9.

Garbarino J, Gilliam G (1980) Understanding Abusive Families. Massachusetts, MN: Lexington Books.

Garrick J (1986) Removing some myths: A comparative study of Australian and migrant families with a child who has disabilities. American Association on Mental Retardation Journal 10(1): 14–16.

Gattai FB, Musatti T (1998) Grandmothers' involvement in grandchildren's care: Attitudes, feelings and emotions. Family Relations 48(1): 35–42.

Geldard D (1998) Basic Personal Counselling. 3rd edn. Sydney: Prentice Hall.

Gilding M (1997) Australian Families: A Comparative Perspective. South Melbourne: Longman.

Ginott H (1972) Teacher and Child. New York: Macmillan.

Glidden LM, Floyd FJ (1997) Disaggregating parental depression and family stress in assessing families of children with developmental disabilities: A multisample analysis. American Journal on Mental Retardation 102(3): 250–66.

Glidden LM, Valliere VM, Herbert SL (1988) Adopted children with mental retardation: Positive family impact. Mental Retardation 26(3): 119–25.

Gonzalez–Mena J (1997) Multicultural Issues in Child Care. 2nd edn. Mountain View, CA: Mayfield.

Gordon T (1970) Parent Effectiveness Training. New York: Plume.

Grant G, Ramcharan P, McGrath M, Nolan M, Keady J (1998) Rewards and gratifications among family caregivers. Journal of Intellectual Disability Research 42(1): 58–71.

Greenberg JS, Seltzer MM, Krauss MW, Kim H-W (1997) The differential effects of social support on the psychological well-being of aging mothers of adults with mental illness or mental retardation. Family Relations 46(4): 383–93.

Greene BF, Norman KR, Searle MS, Daniels M, Lubeck RC (1995) Child abuse and neglect by parents with disabilities: A tale of two families. Journal of Applied Behavior Analysis 28(4): 417–34.

Greenman J, Stonehouse A (1997) Prime Times: A Handbook for Excellence in Infant and Toddler Programs. South Melbourne: Longman.

Greer G (1999) The Whole Woman. London: Doubleday.

Grimshaw P (1983) The Australian family: An historical interpretation. In Burns A, Bottomley G, Jools P, (Eds) The Family in the Modern World. Sydney: Allen and Unwin. pp.31–48.

Guralnick MJ (1991) The next decade of research on the effectiveness of early intervention. Exceptional Children 58(2): 174–83.

Hadden S, Fowler SA (1997) Preschool: A new beginning for children and parents. Teaching Exceptional Children 30(1): 36–39.

Hamre-Nietupski S, Krajewski L, Nietupski J, Ostercamp D, Sensor K, Opheim B (1988) Parent/professional partnerships in advocacy: Developing integrated options with resistive systems. Journal for the Association for Persons with Severe Handicaps 13(4): 251–59.

Hannah ME, Midlarsky E (1999) Competence and adjustment of siblings with mental retardation. American Journal on Mental Retardation 104(1): 22–37.

Hanson MJ (1987) Early intervention for children with Down syndrome. In Pueschel SM, Tingey C, Rynders JE, Crocker AC, Crutcher DM, (Eds) New Perspectives on Down Syndrome. Baltimore, MD: Paul H Brooks. pp. 149–70.

Hanson MJ, Carta JJ (1995) Addressing the challenges of families with multiple risks. Exceptional Children 62(3): 201–12.

Harris VS, McHale SM (1989) Family life problems, daily caregiving activities, and the psychological well-being of mothers of mentally retarded children. American Journal on Mental Retardation 94(3): 231–39.

Harrison M (1993) Family Law and Marriage Breakdown in Australia. Melbourne: Australian Institute of Family Studies.

Harry B (1996) These families, those families: The impact of researcher identities on the research act. Exceptional Children 62(4): 292–300.

Harry B, Day M, Quist F (1998) 'He can't really play': An ethnographic study of sibling acceptance and interaction. Journal of the Association for Persons with Severe Handicaps 23(4): 289–99.

Harvey E (1999) Short-term and long-term effects of early parental employment on children of the National Longitudinal Survey of Youth. Developmental Psychology 35(2): 445–59.

Hassiotis A (1997) Parents of young persons with learning disability: An application of the family adaptability and cohesion scale (FACES II). The British Journal of Developmental Disabilities 43(1): 42–47.

Haveman M, van Berkum G, Reijnders R, Heller T (1997) Differences in service needs, time demands, and caregiving burden among parents of persons with mental retardation across the life cycle. Family Relations 46(4): 417–25.

Hayes A (1998) Families and disabilities: Another facet of inclusion. In Ashman A, Elkins J, (Eds) Educating Children with Special Needs. 3rd edn. Sydney: Prentice Hall. pp. 39–66.

Hayes S (1990) Guidelines. In Butler S (Ed) The Exceptional Child. Sydney: Harcourt Brace Jovanovich. pp. 611–20.

Heath HE (1994) Dealing with difficult behaviors: Teachers plan with parents. Young Children 49(5): 20–24.

Helff CM, Glidden LM (1998) More positive or less negative?: Trends in research on adjustment of families rearing children with developmental disabilities. Mental Retardation 36(6): 457–64.

Heller KW, Gallagher PA, Fredrick LD (1999) Parents' perceptions of siblings' interactions with the brothers and sisters who are deaf-blind. Journal for the Association for Persons with Severe Handicaps 24(1): 33–43.

Heller T, Hsieh K, Rowitz L (1997) Maternal and paternal caregiving of persons with mental retardation across the lifespan. Family Relations 46(4): 407–15.

Helm DT, Miranda S, Angoff-Chedd N (1998) Prenatal diagnosis of Down syndrome: Mothers' reflections on supports needed from diagnosis to birth. Mental Retardation 36(1): 55–61.

Hodapp. RM, Fidler DJ, Smith ACM (1998) Stress and coping in families of children with Smith-Magenis syndrome. Journal of Intellectual Disability Research 42(5): 331–40.

Hodapp. RM, Freeman SFN, Kasari CL (1998) Parental educational preferences for students with mental retardation: Effects of etiology and current placement. Education and Training in Mental Retardation and Developmental Disabilities 33(4): 342–49.

Honey C (1991) Whose interests are we protecting: The child's, the family's or the professional's? Australian Journal of Early Childhood 16(1): 22–23.

Honig AS (1986) Stress and coping in children (Part 1). Young Children 41(4): 50–63.

Hornby G (1994) Effects of children with disabilities on fathers: A review and analysis of the literature. International Journal of Disability, Development and Education 41(3): 171–84.

Hostetler L (1991) Collaborating on behalf of children. Young Children 46(2): 2–3.

Howes C (1990) Can the age of entry into child care and the quality of child care predict adjustment in kindergarten? Developmental Psychology 26(2): 292–303.

Huber CH (1994) Ethical, Legal, and Professional Issues in the Practice of Marriage and Family Therapy. 2nd edn. New York: Macmillan.

Hughes D, May D (1988) From child to adult: The significance of school-leaving for the families of adolescents with mental handicaps. In Horobin G, May D (Eds) Living with Mental Handicaps: Transitions in the Lives of People with Mental Handicaps. London: Jessica Kingsley. pp. 94–100.

Hutchins MP, Renzaglia A (1998) Interviewing families for effective transition to employment. Teaching Exceptional Children 30(4): 72–78.

Jakubowski P, Lange AJ (1978) The Assertive Option: Your Rights and Responsibilities. Chicago, IL: Research Press.

Johnson DE, Bullock CC, Ashton-Shaeffer C (1997) Families and leisure: A context for learning. Teaching Exceptional Children 30(2): 30–34.

Judge SL (1998) Parental coping and strengths in families of young children with disabilities. Family Relations 47(3): 263–68.

Katz LG (1995) Talks with Teachers of Young Children. Norwood, NJ: Ablex.

Koegel RL, Shriebman L, Loos LM, Dirlich-Wilhelm H, Dunlap G, Robbins FR, Plienis AJ (1992) Consistent stress profiles in mothers of children with autism. Journal of Autism and Developmental Disorders 22(2): 205–16.

Kraemer BR, Blacher J, Marshal MP (1997) Adolescents with severe disabilities: Family, school and community inclusion. Journal of the Association for Persons with Severe Handicaps 22(4): 224–34.

Kravetz S, Nativitz R, Katz S (1993) Parental coping styles and the school adjustment of children who are mentally retarded. The British Journal of Developmental Disabilities 39(1): 51–59.

Kurtz G, Kurtz PD (1987) Child abuse and neglect. In Neisworth JT, Bagnato SJ, (Eds) The Young Exceptional Child: Early Development and Education. New York: Macmillan. pp. 206–90.

Landesman S, Krauss M, Simeonsson RJ (1989) Research on families: Current assessment and future opportunities. American Journal on Mental Retardation 94(3): ii–vi.

Leach P (1994) Children First. London: Michael Joseph.

Lehmann JP, Roberto KA (1996) Comparison of factors influencing mothers' perceptions about the futures of their adolescent children with and without disabilities. Mental Retardation 34(1): 27–38.

Llewellyn G (1990) People with intellectual disability as parents: Perspectives from the professional literature. Australia and New Zealand Journal of Developmental Disabilities 16(4): 369–80.

Llewellyn G (1994) Generic family support services: Are parents with learning disability catered for? Mental Handicap Research 7(1): 64–77.

Llewellyn G (1995) Relationships and social support: Views of parents with mental retardation/intellectual disability. Mental Retardation 33(6): 349–63.

Llewellyn G, Brigden D (1995) Factors affecting service provision to parents with intellectual disability: An exploratory study. Australia and New Zealand Journal of Developmental Disabilities 20(2): 97–112.

Llewellyn G, Dunn P, Fante M, Turnbull L, Grace R (1999a) Family factors influencing out-of-home placement decisions. Journal of Intellectual Disability Research 43(3): 219–33.

Llewellyn G, Thompson K, Proctor A (1999b) Early intervention services and parents with disabilities. International Journal of Practical Approaches to Disability 23(1): 3–8.

Lobato D (1983) Siblings of handicapped children: A review. Journal of Autism and Developmental Disorders 13(4): 347–64.

Lobato D (1990) Brothers, Sisters and Special Needs. Baltimore, MD: Paul H Brookes.

Lopez A (1996) Creation is ongoing: Developing a relationship with non-English speaking parents. Child Care Information Exchange 107: 56–59.

Lovitt TC, Cushing S (1999) Parents of youth with disabilities: Their perspectives of school programs. Remedial and Special Education 20(3): 134–42.

Lusthaus E, Lusthaus C (1993) A 'normal life' for Hannah: Trying to make it possible. In Turnbull AP, Patterson JM, Behr SK, Murphy DL, Marquis JG, Blue-Banning MJ (Eds) Cognitive Coping, Families and Disability. Baltimore, MD: Paul H Brookes. pp. 43–50.

Luthar SS, Zigler E (1991) Vulnerability and competence: A review of the research on resilience in childhood. American Journal of Orthopsychiatry 6: 6–22.

Mackay H (1994) Why Don't People Listen? Sydney: Pan MacMillan.

MacMullin CE, Napper M (1993) Teachers and inclusion of students with disabilities: Attitude, confidence or encouragement? Paper presented to the Australian Early Intervention Association (SA Chapter) Conference (June 1993), Adelaide.

McCartney JR, Campbell VA (1998) Confirmed abuse cases in public residential facilities for persons with mental retardation: A multi-site study. Mental Retardation 36(6): 465–73.

McConnell D, Llewellyn G, Bye R (1997) Providing services for parents with intellectual disability: Parent needs and service constraints Journal of Intellectual and Developmental Disability, 22 (1): 5–17.

McCubbin HI, McCubbin MA (1988) Typologies of resilient families: Emerging roles of social class and ethnicity. Family Relations 37(3): 247–54.

McDonald P (1993) Family Trends and Structure in Australia. Melbourne: Australian Institute of Family Studies.

McKenzie S (1993) Consultation with parents of young children with disabilities regarding their perception of children's services and service professionals and their needs associated with access and participation in generic children's services. Unpublished Masters Dissertation: Flinders University of South Australia.

McKenzie S (1994) Parents of young children with disabilities: Their perceptions of generic children's services and service professionals. Australian Journal of Early Childhood 19(4): 12–17.

McKenzie S (1995) Perceptions of parents of young children with disabilities about their own quality of life. In Conference Proceedings: 9th Annual Conference Early Intervention of South Australia Inc (August 1995). Adelaide: Early Intervention Association of SA (Inc).

McKenzie S (1996) An interpretive study of quality of life for people who have young children with disabilities. Unpublished doctoral thesis. Adelaide: Flinders University of South Australia.

McKim MK (1993) Quality child care: What does it mean for individual infants, parents and caregivers? Early Child Development and Care 88: 23–30.

McLoughlin JA, Lewis RB (1994) Assessing Special Students. 4th edn. New York: Merrill.

Madanes C (1981) Strategic Family Therapy. San Francisco, CA: Jossey-Bass.

Mahoney G, O'Sullivan PS, Dennebaum J (1990) A national study of mothers' perceptions of family-focused intervention. Journal of Early Intervention 14(2): 133–46.

Mallory B (1996) The role of social policy in life-cycle transitions. Exceptional Children 62(3): 213–23.

Mannis VS (1999) Single mothers by choice. Family Relations 48(2): 121–28.

Mardiros M (1982) Mothers of disabled children: A study of parental stress. Nursing Papers: Perspectives in Nursing 14(3): 47–56.

Martin G Pear J (1999) Behavior Modification: What it is and How to do it. 6th edn. Upper Saddle River, NJ: Prentice-Hall.

Masino LL, Hodapp. RM (1996) Parental educational expectations for adolescents with disabilities. Exceptional Children 62(6): 515–23.

Meyer DJ (1993) Lessons learned: Cognitive coping strategies of overlooked family members. In Turnbull AP, Patterson JM, Behr SK, Murphy DL, Marquis JG, Blue-Banning M J, (Eds) Cognitive Coping, Families and Disability. Baltimore, MD: Paul H Brookes. pp. 81–93.

Minnes PM (1988) Family resources and stress associated with having a mentally retarded child. American Journal on Mental Retardation 93(2): 184–92.

Minnes P, McShane J, Forkes S, Green S, Clement B, Card L (1989) Coping resources of parents of developmentally handicapped children living in rural communities. Australia and New Zealand Journal of Developmental Disabilities 15(2): 109–18.

Mirfin-Veitch B, Bray A, Watson M (1997) 'We're just that sort of family': Intergenerational relationships in families including children with disabilities. Family Relations 46(3): 305–11.

Mitchell-Copeland J, Denham SA, DeMulder EK (1997) Q-sort assessment of child-teacher attachment relationships and social competence in preschool. Early Education and Development 8(1): 27–39.

Mori AA (1983) Families of Children with Special Needs. Gaithersburg, MD: Aspen.

Morningstar ME, Turnbull AP, Turnbull HR III (1995) What do students with disabilities tell us about the importance of family involvement in the transition from school to adult life? Exceptional Children 62(3): 249–60.

Mullins JB (1987) Authentic voices from parents of exceptional children. Family Relations 36(1): 30–33.

Murray-Harvey R, Slee PT (1998) Family stress and school adjustment: Predictors across the school years. Early Child Development and Care 145: 133–49.

National Association for the Education of Young Children (1989) Code of ethical conduct. Young Children 45(1): 25–29.

Nelson-Jones R (1988) Practical Counselling and Helping Skills. New York: Holt, Rinehart and Winston.

Nitschke D (1994) An examination of perceived needs of families with children who have Down syndrome: A description of views from parents and service providers. Unpublished Masters Dissertation. Adelaide: Flinders University of South Australia.

Norris C, Closs A (1999) Child and parent relationships with teachers in schools responsible for the education of children with serious medical conditions. British Journal of Special Education 26(1): 29–33.

O'Brien M, Roy C, Jacobs A, Macaluso M, Peyton V (1999) Conflict in the dyadic play of 3-year-old children. Early Education and Development 10(3): 289–13.

O'Halloran JM (1993) Welcome to our family, Casey Patrick. In Turnbull AP, Patterson JM, Behr SK, Murphy DL, Marquis JG, Blue-Banning MJ, (Eds) Cognitive Coping, Families and Disability. Baltimore, MD: Paul H Brookes. pp. 19-29.

Olshansky, S (1962) Chronic sorrow: A response to having a mentally defective child. Social Casework 43: 190–93.

Padeliadu S (1998) Time demands and experienced stress in Greek mothers of children with Down's syndrome. Journal of Intellectual Disability Research 42(2): 144–53.

Palmer DS, Borthwick-Duffy SA, Widaman K (1998a) Parent perceptions of inclusive practices for their children with significant cognitive disabilities. Exceptional Children 64(2): 271–82.

Palmer DS, Borthwick-Duffy SA, Widaman K, Best SJ (1998b) Influences on parent perceptions of inclusive practices for their children with mental retardation. American Journal on Mental Retardation 103(3): 272–87.

Patterson JM (1991) Family resilience to the challenge of a child's disability. Pediatric Annals 20(9): 491–500.

Pearson S (1996) Child abuse among children with disabilities. Teaching Exceptional Children 29(1): 34–37.

Perry A, Sarlo-McGarvey N, Factor DC (1992) Stress and family functioning in parents of girls with Rett syndrome. Journal of Autism and Developmental Disorders 22(2): 235–48.

Peterson NL, Cooper CS (1989) Parent education and involvement in early intervention programs for handicapped children: A different perspective on parent needs and parent-professional relationships. In Fine MJ, (Ed) The Second Handbook on Parent Education. New York: Academic. pp. 197–234.

Pope KS (1988) How clients are harmed by sexual contact with mental health professionals: The syndrome and its prevalence. Journal of Counseling and Development 67: 222–26.

Porter L (1999) Behaviour management practices in child care centres. Unpublished doctoral thesis. Adelaide: University of South Australia.

Powell T, Gallagher P (1993) Brothers and Sisters: A Special Part of Exceptional Families. 2nd edn. Baltimore, MD: Paul H Brookes.

Pruchno RA, Patrick JH, Burant CJ (1996) Aging women and their children with chronic disabilities: Perceptions of sibling involvement and effects on well-being. Family Relations 45(3): 318–26.

Raban B (1997) What counts towards quality provision? International Journal of Early Childhood 29(1): 57–63.

Raines S (1995) Never Ever Serve Sugary Snacks on Rainy Days: The Official Little Instruction Book for Teachers of Young Children. Beltsville, MD: Gryphon House.

Rasmussen L (1993) Quality of life for parents of a child with a developmental disability. Unpublished Masters thesis. Calgary, AB: University of Calgary.

Rekers GA (1984) Ethical issues in child behavioral assessment. In Ollendick TH, Hersen M, (Eds) Child Behavioral Assessment. New York: Pergamon. pp. 244–62.

Rimmerman A, Duvdevany I (1995) Coping resources of mothers of integrated and non-integrated pre-schoolers with developmental disabilities. The British Journal of Developmental Disabilities 41(1): 42–47.

Rimmerman A, Kramer R, Levy JM, Levy PH (1989) Who benefits most from respite care? International Journal of Rehabilitation Research 12(1): 41–47.

Robbins FR, Dunlap G, Plienis AJ (1991) Family characteristics, family training, and the progress of young children with autism. Journal of Early Intervention 15(2): 173–84.

Roberts RN, Rule S, Innocenti MS (1998) Strengthening the Family-Professional Partnership in Services for Young Children. Baltimore, MD: Paul H Brookes.

Roe D (1988) Siblings of the disabled. Australian Journal of Early Childhood 13(2): 39–41.

Rogers C (1942) Counseling and Psychotherapy: Newer Concepts in Practice. Boston, MA: Houghton Mifflin.

Ronai CR (1997) On loving and hating my mentally retarded mother. Mental Retardation 35(6): 417–32.

Rosin P (1996a) Parent and service provider partnerships in early intervention. In Rosin P, Whitehead AD, Tuchman LI, Jesien GS, Begun AL, Irwin L, (Eds) Partnerships in Family-Centred Care: A Guide to Collaborative Early Intervention. Baltimore, MD: Paul H Brookes. pp. 65–79.

Rosin P (1996b) The diverse American family. In Rosin P, Whitehead AD, Tuchman LI, Jesien GS, Begun AL, Irwin L, (Eds) Partnerships in Family-Centred Care: A Guide to Collaborative Early Intervention. Baltimore, MD: Paul H Brookes. pp. 3–28.

Rosin P, Whitehead AD, Tuchman LI, Jesien GS, Begun AL, Irwin L (1996) Partnerships in Family-Centred Care: A Guide to Collaborative Early Intervention. Baltimore, MD: Paul H Brookes.

Rowe H (1990) Testing and evaluation of persons with handicap. In Butler S (Ed) The Exceptional Child. Sydney: Harcourt Brace Jovanovich. pp. 543–68.

Rutter M (1985) Resilience in the face of adversity: Protective factors and resistance to psychiatric disorder. British Journal of Psychiatry 147: 598–611.

Ryan NM (1989) Stress-coping strategies identified from school age children's perspective. Research in Nursing and Health 12(2): 111–22.

Ryndak DL, Downing JE, Morrison AP, Williams LJ (1996) Parents' perceptions of educational settings and services for children with moderate or severe disabilities. Remedial and Special Education 17(2): 106–18.

Salisbury CL (1990) Characteristics of users and non-users of respite care. Mental Retardation 28(5): 291–97.

Sandler AG (1998) Grandparents of children with disabilities: A closer look. Education and Training in Mental Retardation and Developmental Disabilities 33(4): 350–56.

Sandler AG, Mistretta LA (1998) Positive adaptation in parents of adults with disabilities. Education and Training in Mental Retardation and Developmental Disabilities 33(2): 123–30.

Schilling RF, Schinke SP, Blythe BJ, Barth RP (1982) Child maltreatment and mentally retarded parents: Is there a relationship? Mental Retardation 20(3): 201–9.

Schilling RF, Kirkham MA, Snow WH, Schinke SP (1986) Single mothers with handicapped children: Different from their married counterparts? Family Relations 35(1): 69–77.

Schonell FJ, Watts BH (1956) A first survey of the effects of a subnormal child on the family unit. American Journal of Mental Deficiency 61: 210–19.

Schulz JB (1993) Heroes in disguise In Turnbull AP, Patterson JM, Behr SK, Murphy DL, Marquis JG, Blue-Banning MJ, (Eds) Cognitive Coping, Families and Disability. Baltimore, MD: Paul H Brookes. pp. 31–41.

Schwarz JC, Krolick G, Strickland RG (1973) Effects of early day care experience on adjustment to a new environment. American Journal of Orthopsychiatry 43(3): 340–46.

Scorgie K, Wilgosh L, McDonald L (1998) Stress and coping in families of children with disabilities: An examination of recent literature. Developmental Disabilities Bulletin 26(1): 22–42.

Sebastian P (1989) Handle With Care: A Guide to Early Childhood Administration. 2nd edn. Milton, QLD: Jacaranda Press.

Sebastian-Nickle P, Milne R (1992) Care and Education of Young Children. Melbourne: Longman Cheshire.

Seligman M (1979) Strategies for Helping Parents of Exceptional Children: A Guide for Teachers. London: Macmillan.

Seligman M, Darling RB (1997) Ordinary Families; Special Children: A Systems Approach to Childhood Disability. 2nd edn. New York: Guilford.

Seligman M, Goodwin G, Paschal K, Applegate A, Lehman, L (1997) Grandparents of children with disabilities: Perceived levels of support. Education and Training in Mental Retardation and Developmental Disabilities 32(4): 293–303.

Seltzer MM, Greenberg JS, Krauss MW, Gordon RM, Judge K (1997) Siblings of adults with mental retardation or mental illness: Effects on lifestyle and psychological well-being. Family Relations 46(4): 395–405.

Sexton D, Lobman M, Constans T, Snyder P, Ernest J (1997) Early interventionists' perspectives of multicultural practices with African-American families. Exceptional Children 63(3): 313–28.

Shertzer B, Stone, S (1974) Fundamentals of Counseling. 2nd edn. Boston, MA: Houghton Mifflin.

Simpson RL (1990) Conferencing Parents of Exceptional Children. 2nd edn. Austin, TX: Pro-Ed Inc.

Singer GHS, Powers LE (Eds) (1993) Families, Disability and Empowerment: Active Coping Skills and Strategies for Family Interventions. Baltimore, MD: Paul H Brookes.

Slee PT (1991) What stresses Australian children? Children Australia 16(3): 12–14.

Smith GC (1997) Aging families of adults with mental retardation: Patterns and correlates of service use, need, and knowledge. American Journal on Mental Retardation 102(1): 13–26.

Smith MJ, Ryan AS (1987) Chinese-American families of children with developmental disabilities: An exploratory study of reactions to service providers. Mental Retardation 25(6): 345–50.

Sobsey D, Mansell S (1997) Teaching people with disabilities to be abused and exploited: The special educator as accomplice. Developmental Disabilities Bulletin 25(1): 77–93.

Sokoly MM, Dokecki PR (1995) Ethical perspectives on family-centred early intervention. In Blackman JA (Ed) Working with Families in Early Intervention. Gaithersburg, MD: Aspen. pp. 186–98.

Solnit AJ, Stark MSS (1961) Mourning and the birth of a defective child. Psychoanalytic Study of the Child 16: 523–37.

Spirito A, Stark LJ, Grace N, Stamoulis D (1991) Common problems and coping strategies reported in childhood and early adolescence. Journal of Youth and Adolescence 20(5): 531–44.

Stainton T, Besser H (1998) The positive impact of children with an intellectual disability on the family. Journal of Intellectual and Developmental Disability 23(1): 57–70.

Stewart JC (1986) Counselling Parents of Exceptional Children. 2nd edn. Columbus, OH: Merrill.

Stonehouse A (1991a) Our Code of Ethics at Work. Watson, ACT: Australian Early Childhood Association.

Stonehouse A (1991b) Opening the Doors: Child Care in a Multi-cultural Society. Watson, ACT: Australian Early Childhood Association.

Stores R, Stores G, Fellows B, Buckley S (1998) Daytime behavior problems and maternal stress in children with Down's syndrome, their siblings, and non-intellectually disabled and other intellectually disabled peers. Journal of Intellectual Disability Research 42(3): 228–37.

Strike KA, Soltis JF (1992) The Ethics of Teaching. 2nd edn. New York: Teachers College Press.

Suarez LM, Baker BL (1997) Child externalizing behaviour and parents' stress: The role of social support. Family Relations 46(4): 373–81.

Summers JA, Behr SK, Turnbull AP (1989) Positive adaptation and coping strengths of families who have children with disabilities. In Singer GHS, Irvin LK, (Eds) Support for Caregiving Families: Enabling Positive Adaptation to Disability. Baltimore, MD: Paul H Brookes. pp. 27–40.

Summers JA, Dell'Oliver C, Turnbull AP, Benson HA, Santelli E, Campbell M, Siegal-Causey E (1990) Examining the individualised family service plan process: What are family and practitioner preferences? Topics in Early Childhood Special Education 10(1): 78–99.

Sussell A, Carr S, Hartman A (1996) Families R us: Building a parent/school partnership. Teaching Exceptional Children 28(4): 53–57.

Szwarc B (1987) Child welfare for the disabled – Is the battle for justice really being fought? Australian Child and Family Welfare 11(2–3): 5–7.

Thompson CL, Rudolph LB (1996) Counseling Children. 4th edn. Pacific Grove, CA: Brookes/Cole.

Thompson L, Lobb C, Elling R, Herman S, Jurkiewicz T, Hulleza C (1997) Pathways to family empowerment: Effects of family-centred delivery of early intervention services. Exceptional Children 64(1): 99–113.

Thorin E, Yovanoff P, Irvin L (1996) Dilemmas faced by families during their young adults' transitions to adulthood: A brief report. Mental Retardation 34(2): 117–20.

Tinworth S (1994) Conceptualising a collaborative partnership between parents and staff in early childhood services. In Mellor EJ, Coombe KM (Eds) Issues in Early Childhood Services: Australian Perspectives. Dubuque, IO: William C Brown. pp. 25–38.

Trivette CM, Dunst CJ, Boyd K, Hamby DW (1996) Family-oriented program models, helpgiving practices, and parental control appraisals. Exceptional Children 62(3): 237–48.

Trute B, Hauch C (1988) Building on family strength: A study of families with positive adjustment to the birth of a developmentally disabled child. Journal of Marital and Family Therapy 14(2): 185–93.

Turnbull AP (1988) The challenge of providing comprehensive support to families. Education and Training in Mental Retardation 23(4): 261–72.

Turnbull AP, Friesen BJ, Ramirez C (1998) Participatory action research as a model for conducting family research. Journal of The Association for Persons with Severe Handicaps 23(3): 178–88.

Turnbull AP, Ruef M (1996) Family perspectives on problem behavior. Mental Retardation 34(5): 280–93.

Turnbull AP, Turnbull HR (1986) Families, Professionals and Exceptionality: A Special Partnership. Columbus, OH: Merrill.

Turnbull AP, Turnbull HR (1990) Families, Professionals and Exceptionality: A Special Partnership. 2nd edn. Upper Saddle River, NJ: Merrill.

Turnbull AP, Turnbull HR (1993) Participatory research on cognitive coping: From concepts to research planning. In Turnbull AP, Patterson JM, Behr SK, Murphy DL, Marquis JG, Blue-Banning MJ, (Eds) Cognitive Coping, Families and Disability. Baltimore, MD: Paul H Brookes. pp. 1–14.

Turnbull AP, Turnbull HR (1997) Families, Professionals and Exceptionality: A Special Partnership. 3rd edn. Upper Saddle River, N J: Merrill.

Turnbull, HR, Guess D, Turnbull AP (1988) Vox Populi and Baby Doe. Mental Retardation 26(3): 127–32.

Tyler B, Dettmann L (1980) Meeting the toddler more than halfway: The behavior of toddlers and their caregivers. Young Children 35(2): 39–46.

Tymchuk AJ (1992) Predicting adequacy of parenting by people with mental retardation. Child Abuse and Neglect 16: 165–78.

Vandell DL, Henderson VK, Wilson KS (1988) A longitudinal study of children with day-care experiences of varying quality. Child Development 59(5): 1286–92.

Voelker S, Shore D, Hakin-Larson J, Bruner D (1997) Discrepancies in parent and teacher ratings of adaptive behavior of children with multiple disabilities. Mental Retardation 35(1): 10–17.

Warfield ME, Hauser-Cram P (1996) Child care needs, arrangements, and satisfaction of mothers of children with developmental disabilities. Mental Retardation 34(5): 294–302.

Waters J (1996) Making the Connection: Parents and Early Childhood Staff. Melbourne: Lady Gowrie Child Centre (Melbourne) Inc.

Waters M, Crook R (1993) Sociology One: Principles of Sociological Analysis for Australians. 3rd edn. Melbourne: Longman.

Webster-Stratton C, Spitzer A (1996) Parenting a young child with conduct problems: New insights using qualitative methods. In Ollendick TH, Prinz RJ (Eds) Advances in Clinical Child Psychology (Vol. 18). New York: Plenum Press. pp. 1–62.

Westling DL (1996) What do parents of children with moderate and severe mental disabilities want? Education and Training in Mental Retardation and Developmental Disabilities 31(2): 86–114.

Westling DL, Plaute W (1999) Views of Austrian parents about special education services for their children with mental disabilities. Education and Training in Mental Retardation and Developmental Disabilities 34(1): 43–57.

Whelan T, Kelly S (1986) A Hard Act to Follow: Step-parenting in Australia Today. Melbourne: Penguin.

Whitman BY, Graves B, Accardo P (1987) Mentally retarded parents in the community: Identification method and needs assessment survey. American Journal of Mental Deficiency 91(6): 636–38.

Whitney-Thomas J, Hanley-Maxwell C (1996) Packing the parachute: Parents' experiences as their children prepare to leave high school. Exceptional Children 63(1): 75–87.

Williams M, Roper S (1985) Community-based respite care for disabled children Australian Child and Family Welfare, 10 (1), 1–4.

Wilson J, Blacher J, Baker BL (1989) Siblings of children with severe handicaps. Mental Retardation 27(3): 167–73.

Yau MK, Li-Tsang CWP (1999) Adjustment and adaptation in parents of children with developmental disability in two-parent families: A review of the characteristics and attributes. The British Journal of Developmental Disabilities 45(1): 38–51.

Yoder PL (1987) Relationship between degree of infant handicap and clarity of infant cues. American Journal of Mental Deficiency 91(6): 639–41.

Zimmerman MA, Arunkumar R (1994) Resiliency research: Implications for schools and policy. Social Policy Report 8(4): 1–17.

Index

DATE DUE

Printed in USA

HIGHSMITH #45230